A Cybercop's Guide to Internet Child Safety

by Glen Klinkhart

www.cybercopguide.com

Dedication

To Evan and to Jay.

To the victims of crime and to the families who refuse to allow tragedy to destroy their lives.

Author – Glen Klinkhart

Glen Klinkhart began his high-tech career at the age of twelve when he received his first book about BASIC Programming.

In 1982, at age fifteen Glen's older sister Dawn was kidnapped, sexually assaulted, and murdered. Through the diligent and dedicated work of law enforcement, Fire Investigators, Medical Examiners, and Prosecutors, Dawn's killer was brought to justice and is serving time for his crimes. The ramification of his sister's murder would resonate within Glen throughout his life and ultimately would lead him to a career in law enforcement, homicide investigation, and cybercrime investigations.

After the murder of his sister, Glen began a career in the computer industry as a technology consultant, computer technician, and instructor. After earning a business degree from Linfield College in Oregon in 1998, he returned to Alaska to work in the high tech industry with computer certification by Hewlett Packard and Apple Computer. In 1995, he became a certified police officer and police detective. In 1998 Glen created the Computer Crime Unit of the Anchorage Police Department and worked as a Police Detective specializing in Internet crimes as well as spending a number of years working in the Homicide Unit. Glen Klinkhart has investigated hundreds of high tech crimes for local and other police departments. He has assisted with investigations for dozens of law enforcement agencies including the Federal Bureau of Investigation, United States Customs and Immigration Service, Secret Service, Immigration and Naturalization Service, U.S. Attorney's office and the Alaska State Troopers.

With over eighteen years in High Tech and Internet crimes, Klinkhart regularly investigates Internet related crimes. He has interviewed people who are responsible for committing these crimes and many of their victims. He regularly trains other police officers in the sciences of computer and Internet crime investigations and is responsible for the development and wide spread use of high-tech tools and techniques used to solve computer-related crimes.

Recognized as an authority in the area of computer and Internet crime investigation, Glen has been the focus of numerous print media articles. He has also appeared on radio and television to include an Edward R. Murrow Award winning television news special "Web Crawlers," a report on Internet predators and Dateline's "Mystery at Bootlegger's Cove." CNN/Time Magazine television has nationally televised his opinions of the future of computer crime and computer crime investigations. He continues to speak to school children and their parents about the topics of Internet child safety and high-tech crime prevention.

Table of Contents

Introduction   1

The Internet... What is it?   5
    Connecting to the Internet   6

The World Wide Web   11
    Connecting to the World Wide Web (WWW) 12

Email   15

Social Networking Sites   19

Chat   23
    Chat Sites   23
    Chat Software   25
    Chat Rooms   27
    Yahoo Instant Messenger   27
    mIRC   32

File Sharing   41
    Gnutella Network   43
    BitTorrent   43

Newsgroups   47
    Connecting to the Newsgroups   47

Cell Phones   51

Your child as a victim   53
    World Wide Web & Your Kids   61
    Pornography   61
    Hate Sites   63
    Anarchists/Bomb recipes   64
    Checking Your Child's Web Activities   69
    Web Caches and Web Histories   69
    C is for Cookie   76
    Internet Filtering and Tracking Software 83
    Internet Filters   83

Search Engine Filters   83
Internet Content Filters at Home   86
Microsoft's Family Safety   88
Installing Family Safety   88
Internet Content Filters at your ISP   101
Domain Names Services (DNS)   101
Internet Tracking Software   107
Email   111
Do your kids have an email account?   112
Email Rules for Families   116
Unsolicited Emails (Spam)   123
How to avoid getting unsolicited email   123
How to curtail unsolicited email   124
Chat rooms   127
Guarding your Child's Personal Information   131
Cyber Bullying   137
What form does the harassment take?   137
What is the extent of the harassment?   138
What is the intent of the harassment?   139
Cyberbullying/Harassment and the Law   142
Internet Stalking and the Law   143
Runaway/Missing Children   147

Children as Prey: The Sexual Assault of Minors   155
Signs your child may be at risk   166
Are your kids using the computer when you are
unaware?   166
Are your kids being sent pornography?   167
What if your child is being groomed by a Predator   169
Searching for Files   170
Searching for Internet Images   170
Searching for files by Date   173

Your child as a perpetrator   187
CyberBullying, and Harassment   191
Pornography   201
Adult Porn Pay Per View   201

Free Porn Sites and Fraud 204
File Sharing – All the free porn you want 206
Pornography and Sexual Exploration 206
Sexting 209
Child Pornography and your kids 211
Computer Intrusion 219
It's not Hacking, it's burglary 219
Things that go bump on the net 221
Scanners 221
Trojan Horses 222
Computer Viruses 224
Denial of Service Attacks 225

Protecting your online family 231
Virus Protection 232
Firewall Protection 233
Hate Sites 243
Anarchists/Bomb recipes 244
Property Crimes 247
Theft 247
Credit Cards 247
Passwords 249
Counterfeiting 257

Protecting your children 261
Setting up rules 261
Protecting your Internet Child at School 265
Does the school have Internet access? 265
Do they have an Acceptable Use Policy? 266
Banner Displays 266
Tracking user name and passwords 266
Logging Internet Connections 267
Internet filters 267
If all else fails 268

Conclusion 269

Appendix A - Resources on the World Wide Web 271

Child Safe Search Engines   271
Child Safety Web Sites   271
Reporting Online Crime   271

Appendix B - Glossary of Internet terms for Parents   273

Appendix C - Internet International Country Codes   297

Index   303

Introduction

Likely you picked up this book because you are interested in keeping your loved ones safe while they are using this wide and wonderful thing called the "Internet." It is your responsibility as parents to know as much as the people who would do harm to your kids while online.

Cops are by their nature the kind of people who like to keep things short, sweet, and to the point. One may recall the classic television police Sergeant Joe Friday declaring "the facts, ma'am, just the facts." Because I was a police investigator for many years, I am going to tell you in the next forty words or so exactly what you need to do to keep your child (or any child in your charge) safe from the Internet. This way you can put this book down, go home, and feel good about your child's safety when it comes to using the Internet.

Ready? Okay, here it is:

"Turn off the Internet, and never, ever allow your child to access a computer, cell phone or the Internet again."

That being said, the rest of this book is for those people who want to live in the real world, who want to understand the Internet and its possible hazards, and who want to learn more about the safeguards and solutions that are available.

Look at your children for a moment. Do you look at them and see a reflection of yourself? Most likely you see your son or daughter as a young person who has their whole life ahead of them. You may look at your kids and see a future doctor, teacher, or maybe an architect. Take a moment and ask yourself, "Have I ever seen my child as a potential victim?" Probably not. In my line of work I often have to do just that. I have to listen to parents whose child is missing and hear the fear that their son or daughter is with someone that they do not know or is with someone whom they met on the Internet. In this book I will ask you to look at your child in ways that you may not have ever thought about. Ways you may not want to think about. Have you ever looked at your child and wondered if they might be a potential criminal? Could he or she be an online perpetrator? Think about that for a minute. I have plenty of experience in arresting children for using the Internet to commit crimes. Many people don't get to see that side of computers and technologies until the police come knocking on their door with an arrest warrant for their fifteen-year-old. You should know that your child can be exposed to things on the Internet that can manipulate them into becoming an online victim or even a potential criminal. And this can be occurring while you are downstairs thinking that your kids were safe and sound in their upstairs bedroom using their computers for "homework."

My intention is not to suggest your child will be a victim, or is a criminal. Rather it is to increase your awareness while providing tools for you and your children. Awareness and choice are powerful allies. I have designed this book so that you can go directly to the subject that you wish to learn about and read what you feel is important to you and your particular situation. If you want to know about chat rooms, then go to the chapter that I appropriately named "Chat Rooms." Want to know about emails? Go to the chapters about "Emails." Nothing too high tech about that I hope. Scattered throughout this book I have placed many actual cases that I have been involved with and investigated. I am not making this stuff up. These cases run the gamut from the scary to the downright bizarre. I have learned from each of these cases and believe reviewing real life situations offers each of us the opportunity to learn and take steps to avoid the mistakes made by others. In many of these cases I have changed the names of those people and places involved to protect their identities and privacy. In other instances I have combined cases both for the sake of efficiency and getting to the heart of the matter. I can assure you, however, that these cases are real, as are the victims and the perpetrators involved.

Technology continues to provide incredible ways to learn and to communicate. Technology, however, brings with it a dark side which some people in our society will wish to take advantage of. Whether you read the entire book or simply use it as a reference, I do hope that you will be able to take from these pages a sense that there are safeguards we can employ that increase the potential for the wellbeing of our children and reduce the likelihood of harm. Some of these solutions are technical in nature; however I believe that you will find most of them require little computer skills and cost little or no money. All it takes is a little time and effort to increase your own awareness so that you are better equipped to protect your kids while they are on the Internet.

The Internet... What is it?

The Internet is the global communication system that links the world's computer networks together. That is what I call the "learned" definition. The Internet grew out of a series of wide area computer networks in the 60s and 70s. These networks included the United State Department of Defense Research and Development Network called the ARPAnet. Over the past forty years or so, more and more computer networks were added to the mix. The Internet is both an electronic infrastructure and a set of rules, which allows the entire system to work. You don't really see it, but it is everywhere you go when you go "online" or on the "Internet." The Internet lets you ask for and receive information in all types of forms including text, pictures, or video. When your home computer connects to your Internet Service Provider (ISP) you are connected with the Internet or as it is sometimes referred to "the Net," "cyberspace," "online," or the "information super highway." From there anything can and usually does happen.

A network is simply two or more computers linked together to share information. The Internet happens to be the world's largest computer network. Think about this for a moment. Right now there are millions and millions of people who have allowed their office and home computers to join the other millions and millions of home and office computers around the world to form an electronic connection. The possibilities for positive, thoughtful, and beneficial communications are endless. But then again, so are the possibilities that you and your kids can be subjected to negative, thoughtless, and destructive online communications from those who are only concerned with their own personal wants and desires.

Connecting to the Internet

Let us take a look and see what is occurring "under the hood" of your computer when you connect to the Internet.

The first thing that your computer does is attempt to establish a link between itself and the Internet. These days the most common method involves your computer attached to a cable or DSL modem. Modem stands for "MOdulator-DEModulator". The modem's job is to establish and convert the signals while maintaining your computer's electronic connection with the Internet. These days your high speed internet uses a cable or DSL modem to connect either through the cable television lines or telephone line (in the case of DSL) to your Internet service provider (or ISP), who in turn connects you to the Internet. An ISP is a company which provides Internet access to individuals and businesses, usually for a monthly fee. The price you will pay per month usually depends on the usage, connection speeds, number of computers, and other various options.

As your cable or DSL modem connects with the Internet Service Provider's network, your home's modem and your Internet account is given an identifying name and number by which the Internet can keep track of who you are. Now before all of you paranoid technophobes get mad and scream about personal privacy and "how dare the Internet keep track of me!" realize that this is simply a naming convention required by the Internet provider when you use it. Your Internet Provider does not tell the entire world that "Mr. Smith is online and he is looking at pictures of nude chickens!" In order for your computer to send and receive information your computer and the Internet has to know where to go and how to get there. It is more akin to you having a physical mailing address. Without a mailing address, the post office, the USP guy, and the FedEx lady can't deliver your stuff to you. The Internet requires an address as well in order to send and receive the information that you have requested.

Once the connection is made with your ISP, your online session is given an Internet Protocol Address (IP address for short). For example, when I connect with my home network via my cable modem to the Internet my ISP issues me IP address of:

66.223.212.125

Interesting number, huh? That little number that I am issued (or leased) is what is required to send and receive information while connected to the Internet. Cable modems stay connected for long periods of time and may have the same IP address for days, weeks, or months. You can also pay your ISP to give you what is called a "static" IP address. Having a static IP address means that you will ALWAYS have a certain IP address. This is necessary if you are running a business on the Internet and people need to always find you in the same place. For example, my son and I often visit the web site for the kids TV and Internet channel of Nickelodeon. I happen to know that the Nickelodeon's web site on the Internet has a static IP address of:

129.228.33.51

The problem for a business like the Nickelodeon Channel (among others) is that it is hard for companies to convince people to come to their web page if every time they want to go to their web site people need to remember a number like 129.228.33.51. People don't respond to numbers very well, especially long boring numbers like an IP address. This is where the concept of Internet Protocol (IP) names comes in. We have all seen them. Internet Protocol names are the ".com" and ".net" names being advertised on almost every television commercial and print ad in the country. The IP name and the IP address are translated into one another, thus making the Internet better able to process these numbers while humans like us can best deal with remembering names.

For example: The IP address 129.228.33.51 translates to
www.nick.com and the name www.nick.com
translates to IP address of 129.228.33.51

www.nick.com is the "domain name" address. The word, "nick" is the name of the address and the .com indicates that the computer is a commercial (com) internet site. I think that most people would agree that it is much easier to remember the name nick.com than the long boring number of 129.228.33.51.

Some of the other domain name extensions that you will see include:

> EDU – USA (Educational)
> GOV – USA (Government)
> ORG – Global (Non-Profit Organization)
> COM – Global (Commercial)

(See also Appendix C- Internet Country Codes for a complete listing of domain extensions)

Remember the IP address I had on my computer? It was 66.223.212.125. My IP address translates to the domain name of"125-212-223-66.gci.net."

Not a very pretty name but it will work for this short example. The Internet connection is made in the area of my home. The "gci" is the name of my Internet Service provider (General Communications Inc), and the .net indicates that it is a "network." Many ISPs are in the .net domain. The number (125-212-223-66) is the original IP address in reverse. Companies use different domain names so the IP domain name that you receive will vary from provider to provider.

To find out what IP address your computer has when connected to the Internet, connect and log onto the Internet as you normally would. This connection may be in the form of a high-speed modem such as cable or DSL using your telephone line. Once you are connected to the Internet you can then check and see what IP address your Internet Service Provider (ISP) gave you.

One quick and easy way to determine what IP address your Internet Provider gave you for the world to see is to go to a website called www.ipchicken.com. There are other web sites and ways to locate your IP address, but this is an easy way to quickly know how the Internet sees you. Simply use your favorite web browser (Internet Explorer, Firefox, Chrome, etc) and go to www.ipchicken.com. Ipchicken will display the IP address for your home or business (Figure 1).

Figure 1

So my current IP address on the Internet is indeed 66.223.212.125.

"So why do I have to know about these IP numbers, domain names, and all that other kind of junk?" The answer is that you may not need to know about them, unless of course your children are being harassed, stalked, or heaven forbid, kidnapped by someone that they met on the Internet. These IP names and addresses may become your only link to tracing and identifying the Internet suspect. That's why you need to know about them. Remember, you could always "Throw away your computer and turn off your Internet service, and never, ever allow your child to access the Internet again."

It is important to also be aware of IP addresses because we are going to learn more about them in the following chapters as they relate to electronic mail (email).

The millions of computers that are attached to the Internet can provide a myriad of services. Some of the more popular Internet services include such things as the World Wide Web (WWW), Newsgroups/Discussion Groups, Chat Rooms, and of course email.

As a parent, it is important that you know where your kids are "hanging out" while on the Internet. In the following chapters let us take a look at each of these areas in more detail and give you an idea of what kinds of things can be found online.

The World Wide Web

When people are asked to describe the Internet they most likely think of the World Wide Web (WWW). The World Wide Web (or web for short) is all of the Internet web sites that you look at when using web programs (or browsers), such as Microsoft's Internet Explorer (Figure 2). The web browser is the program, or application, that you use to travel Internet web pages by entering a "www.something.com" address.

Internet Explorer

Figure 2

Internet Explorer is free and comes with your Microsoft Windows Operating System. Internet Explorer is not the only web browsing program. There are many other web browsers for Microsoft Windows and Apple Macintosh operating Systems. Such programs include, but are not limited to:

Firefox

Chrome

Safari

11

Opera

Connecting to the World Wide Web (WWW)

With web-browsing programs such as Internet Explorer or Firefox you can type the address of:

www.nick.com

This address will get you to the Nickelodeon Channel's wonderful and web-safe Internet pages for kids. I suspect that 80% of you out there have been using web browsers and "surfing" the web thinking that web pages was what the Internet was all about. The World Wide Web is an excellent service, however, please be aware that it is not the entire realm of the Internet (trust me your kids likely already know this). The World Wide Web's ease of use, visual pages, searchable text, graphics, sounds and mouse "clickable" links to other web pages has made the web (WWW) the most widely used portion of the Internet. It wasn't until the world wide web (WWW) came along that the Internet became so very popular.

When you visit a web site there are several things that you should be aware of that will happen. When you type www.nick.com your computer goes out onto the Internet and attempts to locate where nick.com is (or you can use and type in what we learned about nick.com's actual IP address of 129.228.33.51 to impress your friends). The Internet request finds nick.com by locating another computer called a Domain Name Server (DNS) which checks against its list of known computer names. The DNS responds to your request for www.nick.com by returning the actual IP address for Nickelodeon's web computer (or server as the techno-geeks call it). In this case, the IP address for Nickelodeon's web server is 129.228.33.51 for more information about IP names and addresses see the earlier chapter entitled "Connecting to the Internet"). With this number your computer is now able to ask the Nickelodeon web computer "Are you really out there?" If the Nickelodeon web site is there, your computer then asks if it has some World Wide Web pages (WWW) to send you. If the computer answers yes to these two questions it then begins the process of sending the pages, including text (words), drawings, photos, sounds, and movies to your computer. When the two computers agree with each other, the transfer of the web pages begins from their IP address to your IP address.

This process may take a few seconds or a few minutes depending on the connection speed of the Nickelodeon computer and of course your connection speed. The information does not come all at once to your computer, rather the data is sent in small pieces called "packets." As the information leaves it goes out in bite sized bits of data. When it arrives at your computer, the packets of data you requested are then re-assembled in the correct order, saved on your computer's hard disk drive, and magically your web pages appear in your web browser's main window. The faster your connection speed is to the Internet the faster the packets will arrive and be reassembled on your computer.

It is important to note the part I just mentioned about the web browser saving the web pages onto your computer's hard disk drive. The web browsers do this because they want to try and be as efficient as possible. Should you go to a web site, such as nick.com, and then go to another site, say disney.com (the Walt Disney Internet Web site for kids) the computer can recall the last site that you went to. After a while you may decide to switch back to the nick.com web site. Rather than taking all that time making nick.com re-send you the nick.com web pages, the web browser checks to see if you recently were at the nick.com site and it then simply gets the web data from your hard drive. It is much faster to pull the old web page information back again from your hard disk drive than to waste the time of the Internet, the nick.com computer, and your computer if we don't have to. This saved, or "cached" web page data can remain on your computer's hard disk drive for some time depending on the web browser you are using and what settings the browser has in it.

At one time hardly anyone had their own web page. Now everyone is getting into the act. This can be a good thing for many different reasons. You can shop for anything and everything while cruising or "surfing" the World Wide Web (WWW). You can buy books (and a lot more) at places like amazon.com or barnesandnoble.com. The World Wide Web made the Internet so easy that anyone, at any age or skill level can now use the Internet. This includes those of us whose intentions are good as well as those among us who are more inclined to act out in evil ways.

I have included a list of web sites that can help you choose where on the Internet you and your children can "surf" and feel relatively safe (see Appendix A: Resources on the World Wide Web- Child Safe Web Resources). I say "relatively" because as cops we are often a little bit paranoid of other people who are around us and our family. This type of paranoia is actually a developed skill and not a mental illness. I highly recommend that parents take the time to learn how to be just a little bit paranoid when it comes to protecting our children. For an excellent series of books about developing warning skills to physically protect yourself and your family out in the real world (as opposed to the Internet or cyber-world that we are discussing here), I highly recommend a series of books by author Gavin De Becker. One of his books *"Protecting the Gift: Keeping Children and Teenagers Safe (and Parents Sane)"* is a particularly excellent read for all parents who worry about someone committing emotional or physical harm to their children.

Email

Emails are lightning fast electronic messages that can be sent from one computer to another. If the person who is being sent the email is not online, they can get their messages the next time they log on. Most emails usually contain text, although you can now send almost anything (pictures, sounds, movies, etc.) via email. The way that the world works and communicates has been changed by email. I have to admit that I love email. I have several email accounts that I check at least twice a day. With the advent of smart cell phones I can check my email anywhere and anytime. I use email to keep in touch with friends, family and with people at work. I also send and receive emails to and from other Cybercops all over the world. I like the fact that I can read my email when and where I want to. I can reply to my emails immediately or return to the message at another time.

Email works because of the Internet's ability to quickly send data from point A to point B. In the case of email there is a starting point, which is the senders email account, and an ending point, which is the recipient's email account.

With most Internet Service Providers, you often receive an email account when you sign up for their service. There are also free email accounts that are very popular and are easy to setup. Popular email systems include:

Hotmail.com
Gmail.com
Yahoo.com

One of the big advantages of the free accounts includes being able to read your emails using the World Wide Web and your favorite web browsers (Internet Explorer, Firefox, etc), anywhere you have access to the Internet.

Your email account usually starts with your Internet user name (like "bobsmith1234") and the name of the company that directs your email (such as hotmail.com, gmail.com, gci.net, etc). Put the two together and you get:

bobsmith1234@hotmail.com or bobsmith1234@gci.net

That is your email address.

To get your own free email address all you have to do is have access to the Internet and have web browsing software such as Internet Explorer or Mozilla Firefox (see the chapter entitled "What is... the World Wide Web"). These services allow you to use a web browser to send and receive emails via the World Wide Web. It is free and easy to set up one of these email accounts. Chances are very good that your kids have a Hotmail, Gmail, or Yahoo email account that you may or may not be aware of. I often lecture to school age children and I am surprised by the number of kids who have these free email accounts without their parent's knowledge. Many children share with me that they have multiple email accounts and in many cases their parents have no idea that these accounts exist.

Okay, let's send an email and see what happens. When you type your email you have to give it some place to go. You need to enter an email address in the "To:" field and your email address is populated automatically into the area marked "From:". The "To:" field is so the email knows where it is going and the "from" is so it knows where it came from (in case there is a problem). You can also enter a subject line about the nature of your email or any other pertinent information in the box marked "Subject:" When you press the send button several things happen. The first thing that happens is that you cannot "take back" or undo an email once it is sent out. This can be quite upsetting to some people who have regrettably sent an email message and later wish that they hadn't pressed the send key.

The next thing the email does is it builds itself what is called an email "header." The email's header is necessary for the email to document out where exactly it is going and how it got to where it did. It converts your friends email address into an Internet Protocol (IP) number that the Internet can understand. The email is then sent out of your computer through the Internet and into your ISP's email server (computer) or the free email site (Hotmail, Gmail, etc). At that next point, the computer (server) adds its own information to the email's header. The email server then hands the email off to the next computer in line with the email's final destination. There usually isn't a direct connection between your email service and your friend's email service so the email bounces from one computer server to another until it arrives at its destination. This is like having to take different connecting airline flights to get from Los Angeles to London. When your email arrives at the other person's email server (computer), the email header records that computer's information. The email server then checks its own email system to see if it has the recipients' email address in its list of known email names. If there is a match then it adds your email to the recipient's inbox where it waits to be read. If no correct email address can be found, the email message uses the header information to send itself back to you and let you know there was a problem.

I can hear it now… "Why do I have to know how email travels on the Internet and all this garbage about email headers?" That is a good question. The reason is that we can use that information when we need to learn the identity of those people who are using email to contact our children and trace it back to its source. It is the same techniques we use as Cybercops to track down the bad guys.

Social Networking Sites

Besides the World Wide Web (WWW) and email, one of the other more prolific areas of Internet use is the "social networking" sites. Social Networking sites work with a web browser and the World Wide Web as their foundation, however, unlike a standard web page, social networking sites leverage the internet's ability to connect people quickly and without any need to meet in person. Social networking sites, like Facebook (www.facebook.com), allow everyday people with little or no working knowledge of computers or the internet, to create their own personal web site, to make connections with millions of people around the world, to send messages, photos, videos, and to interact in ways never before available (Figure 3)..

Social Networking sites create instant electronic connections with people and allow us to interact with each other using text, pictures, movies and sound instantly around the world. Such sites have made our ability to connect with other people so much faster and easier. Anyone can set up an account on a social networking site like Facebook and in a few minutes have a finished web page with their name, photos, and entire personal background created for the world to see. With a few clicks of the mouse connections are made with friends, family or with millions of people that you have never personally met.

Figure 3

My Facebook page above shows you the kinds of information that a person can place on a social networking site. You might imagine tools like this can be a wonderful way to connect and interact with people and to enhance one's life. On the other hand, social networking sites are now one of the most popular ways that you and your children can be contacted by people who mean to do harm. These people can now find and attempt to contact your child with just a few clicks of a mouse. Instead of worrying about the finite number of people that your children might meet in their daily activities (school, sports, friends and family gatherings), if your kids have a social network account, you must be aware of the millions of people who now potentially have access to your child.

There are hundreds of different social networking sites. Some of the more popular ones that you should be aware of include:

Facebook (www.facebook.com)

Google+

Google+ (plus.google.com)

Myspace (www.myspace.com)

Myyearbook (www.myyearbook.com)

Many of these sites allow children as young as 13 years of age to set up an account and begin interacting with other people online. They offer web pages, online chatting, messages, and even live video conferencing. Social Networking site provide all of these services for free.

It is important to know if your child has a social networking page and to be able to monitor it. If you allow your child to interact on a social networking site you should be able to see it and be able to monitor who their online "friends" are. One good rule is that your child should not allow anyone that they do not know personally to be one of their online social connections, or "friends".

Chat

Chatting as it relates to the Internet is an electronic connection between two or more computers that allows the participants to communicate through a live typed correspondence. That simply means that people are using their computers to communicate in real time and one-on-one (or in groups) using the Internet. Sometimes people are using software to communicate via the keyboard (typing), although now most chat programs and chat rooms allow for instant video conferencing. All that is necessary to video conferencing is a computer, or cell phone with a camera, and a high speed Internet connection. Video chat has been made easy with sites like Skype offering free video conferencing. In addition, most of the social networking sites now offer various video chatting, including Facebook and GooglePlus.

Chat rooms are Internet meeting areas. These specific areas of the Internet allow two or more people to connect and communicate in one place or a "room" as it is often called. These rooms are found in various areas of the Internet and are often unregulated or are monitored with little or no supervision.

Chat on the Internet has become a big thing. It seems that everyone, including your kids, is spending a great deal of time chatting online using their computers at home, at school, and even on their cellular telephones. I'll leave you my personal opinions regarding chat for a little later on in this book, but for now let's take a look at some of the many different areas of Internet Chat.

Chat Sites

Chat sites are becoming more and more popular. It seems that every internet site out there is offering some version of chatting.

Even shopping sites are providing live chat with users interested in talking with each other about shopping. You can now even chat with some customer service representative when you have online questions or complaints.

Email sites such as Hotmail, Gmail, and Yahoo mail also provide chat capabilities along with their free email services.

Many of the social networking sites offer chat in live text and video conferencing. Facebook has its live instant chat and has added a new Video Calling service (in conjunction with Skype).

Google's new Google+ social networking site also offers free video chat using what they call "Hangouts." For uses of the Google+ social network, Hangouts are multiple video feeds that you can create in Google+ allowing the user to video chat with as many as nine of their friends (Figure 4).

Figure 4
Google + Hangout creation

Chat Software

There is now a huge market for chat and chat software. There are dozens and dozens of free chat software applications offered by various software companies.

Yahoo Messenger (http://messenger.yahoo.com)

Windows Live Messenger
(http://explore.live.com/windows-live-messenger)

AOL Instant Messenger (AIM) (http://www.aim.com)

Skype (http://www.skype.com)

Google Talk (http://www.google.com/talk/)

ICQ (http://www.icq.com)

mIRC (http://www.mirc.com)

Twitter (http://twitter.com/)

I mention Twitter, which although isn't by definition true chat, but more of a form of broadcasting communication via short text messages. Twitter allows an account user to send short text type messages to hundreds, if not millions, of other people who subscribe to your Twitter feed via the Internet.

There are also other additional software programs designed to allow one person to manage multiple chat accounts through one chat application. Such chat managers include:

Digsby (http://www.digsby.com)

Trillian (http://www.trillian.im)

Adium (Mac OS X) (http://adium.im)

Chat Rooms

Specific rooms for people to meet and chat in are available in every topic that you can imagine. Chat rooms have the potential to increase communication between people, and are designed as specific meeting places by different users and groups for a wide variety of reasons. Participants may be very far apart geographically and benefit by being able to stay in contact with their friends and family. More and more businesses see chat and the use of a chat room as a way to increase communications between employees while saving time and money flying people around the country for meetings. The other side of the technology coin is that chatting and chat rooms allow direct access to you and your children by people that you may not want to be involved with. Online predators themselves will use chat rooms to meet with other predators to exchange information and to learn techniques about how and where to victimize others. In chat rooms, predators are able to teach each other a variety of things, such as how not to get caught, and what to do if they do get caught. They will often trade and sell photographs and movies made of their victims to other criminals. Online chatting is also a great way to meet new victims and get to know their young potential victims without all those nosey parents hanging around.

Yahoo Instant Messenger

The fine folks at Yahoo! (www.yahoo.com) have created their chat application and yahoo web site with ease of use in mind. Yahoo also has its own Internet Search functions email and even games. All you need to do to get started with Yahoo chatting is to go to yahoo.com and create a free account. Once you have created a user name and a password, you can download the Yahoo Instant

Messenger for free at:

http://messenger.yahoo.com/download

Once installed the Yahoo Instant Messenger will become a part of your Windows Toolbar and once you open it and log in you will see your Yahoo Messenger application (Figure 5).

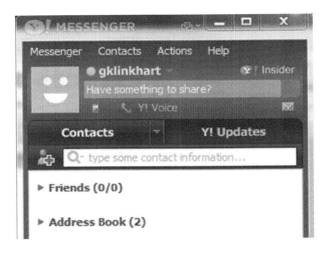

Figure 5

From here you can search for friends (and strangers) to talk to one on one with. Yahoo Messenger will even link your Facebook account, allowing you to see your Facebook status updates and chat with your Facebook friends.

Another feature of Yahoo Messenger is found in their wide variety of chat "rooms." You can access any number of chat rooms by simply clicking on one of interest and within seconds you can begin communicating with hundreds of people from around the world that are of similar interest.

To enter a Yahoo chat room, simply log into your Yahoo Messenger account application and select "Join a Room..." from the Messenger pull down menu (Figure 6).

Figure 6

Next you can choose from any number of chat rooms, including Business, Computers, Hobbies and even chat rooms specific to your region of the world (Figure 7).

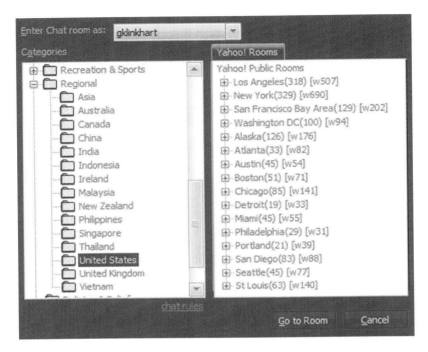

Figure 7

Once in a chat room, you can instantly begin typing away with people from around the world. In the chat room below (Figure 8) there are twenty five people. Everything typed in the room is visible to everyone.

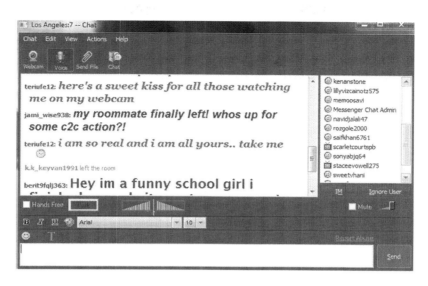

Figure 8

The conversation above quickly moved to sexual chat and even directed chat room users to adult web sites. Within a few minutes of entering the chat room, I was asked by several people to begin a private chat. A private chat is a one on one chat between people and is not seen by the members of the group. I was asked by one of the chat room members for my "asl" or Age, Sex, and Location. This is one way of trying to look for children and to determine their age, gender, and their geographic location. Yahoo chats and chat rooms are designed by Yahoo to only have people older than 18 years of age signed up for them, however since Yahoo accounts are free to set up and kids often lie about their real age during the account creation process, there are many children using Yahoo and other popular chat systems.

The other chat program such as Microsoft Messenger, AOL Instant Messenger, etc, work very much the same way. Many are just as easy to install, operate and are free to download.

31

mIRC

mIRC is one of several computer programs (or clients) for the Windows operating system that allows you to connect with another worldwide chat system known as the Internet Relay Chat (IRC). Other IRC programs include PIRCH (www.pirchat.com) for Windows and Ircle (www.ircle.com) for the Macintosh operating system.

The IRC itself is made up of many different Internet Relay Chat computers or servers as they are often called. Each server allows users to connect to it and in turn, it will connect to the hundreds (or thousands) of other IRC servers around the world. The IRC is broken down into subgroups of networks, the most popular of which are called DALnet, Efnet, Undernet, and IRCnet. There are hundreds of other IRC networks that are available on the Internet.

At any one time there are hundreds of thousands of people using the IRC to chat, join chat rooms and exchange computer files. One can join a one-on-one chat with another person using Direct Client Connections (DCC) chat (Figure 9), join groups (using the /join command), as well as send and receive data (including voice, video, graphics and programs).

Figure 9

No single company or person owns or completely controls the IRC. This fact tends to make the IRC an area of the Internet that operates more like the wild west than a structured or corporate setting found in the Yahoo and the other corporate owned chat areas (although they too are to be used cautiously). All of these chat rooms have the potential to increase communication between people that do not know one another and that may be posing as someone else, to include your own child posing as an adult.

From the CyberCop Case Files:
I Want to Grab a Kid

Once upon a time, a friend of mine with the Federal Bureau of Investigations (FBI) called me with a request. In our part of the country local, state and federal law enforcement officers have to work together because we each have a large area to cover and we are all working with limited resources. The same goes for the local Cybercops. We get together regularly or we call each other in order to discuss the latest high tech crime fighting techniques and we often work cases together. This call from my FBI friend was just a little different. The Special Agent said that he had something new from one of their offices in Texas. He told me that he had received a transcript from an Internet Relay Chat (IRC) session and he wanted to tell me about it. During the IRC chat correspondence one of the participants had written a detailed plan about his preparation to kidnap and rape a young boy from a shopping mall. The chat indicated that the mall might be somewhere in our city. The FBI agent asked if I would be interested in reading the chat session logs to provide him with my opinion of the situation.

When the agent arrived I took a look at the transcript and was horrified by what I read. The IRC chat session showed what appeared to be two people chatting online. One was "PITH," who apparently sent the FBI the computer chat logs, and the other was the suspect known only as "Kimmo."

PITH stated that he and Kimmo began chatting around 4:30 a.m. The conversation lasted approximately 20 minutes at which time PITH became quite concerned about what Kimmo had been telling him. PITH saved the chat log file and then contacted law enforcement about the incident. The chat was a chilling and frightening view into a demented mind.

Kimmo: I'd do a 2yo if I could get away
                with it.
                why not snatch one [a boy] ?
                rape him.

PITH: I could not live with myself.

Kimmo: I know the feeling.
                But I want to do it anyway.
                He'd be 6 or so.

PITH: How young would you go?

Kimmo: newborn I guess, 2 is sweet.

PITH: how long do u think it would
                take b4 u could

	go all the way [with your plan]?
Kimmo:	a few weeks I guess. Take him to the cabin.

The rest of the eight pages of chat noted extremely graphic sexually explicit details which included the very specific ways that the suspect said he would enjoy "raping" and "torturing" his victim. During the rest of the chat the suspect, Kimmo, gave details about the specific shopping mall that he had scoped out and the general area of his cabin north of the city. Kimmo was also very specific about the sexual acts that he was going to perpetrate against his victim. It was apparent that Kimmo had been planning this attack for some time.

It appeared to me that Kimmo had developed a specific plan and additionally it was likely he possessed the ways and means of carrying it out. Although he did not say what he was going to do with the boy after he raped him at the cabin, the details in every other aspect of his plan led me to believe that he did not intend to send the child home alive. Our Crimes Against Children investigators concurred with my analysis and echoed the feeling that this guy was for real and should be taken seriously. We knew that we had to move before Kimmo was able to carry out his plan. The FBI and I immediately began working on the case. At one point we had fourteen agents and police detectives working upon this single investigation. We put officers in the area of the named shopping mall on alert. Every call of a late or a missing child was to be sent directly to me at any time of the day or night. During the course of the week we continued to track and identify the suspect. Three times I was paged that a boy near the area of the mall had been reported late or was missing. In every one of the incidents the children were located quickly and with no signs of foul play. Our luck appeared to be holding, at least for the time being.

We continued to track the location of our suspect by going undercover into Internet Chat rooms looking for Kimmo, tracing his Internet Protocol (IP) address, and using tools such as search warrants and subpoenas to gather a trail of information that could lead to our suspect.

The trail led to a divorced father living on the outskirts of the city. Agents began watching him and his house. Others checked into his background and learned more about how he operated. He appeared to have no criminal history and he was very adept at computers. He also matched many of the details that had been communicated to PITH during the disturbing chat session.

On a clear, cold morning we visited the office and the house of our suspect with our search warrants for both locations. Another group of officers interviewed suspected Kimmo. He played like he didn't know what was being talked about, denying any knowledge of the chat session with PITH. When presented with the irrefutable evidence to include an electronic trail that lead directly to his home computer, he finally admitted that he was Kimmo. He stated that he participated in the chat because he was heavily intoxicated at the time. He told investigators that he had never harmed a child and that he would never hurt anyone.

His computer systems at home and at work told another tale. On his home computer and on various computer media I found hundreds of images of child pornography, including images of children being forced into bondage, and raped. Kimmo had also developed a fondness for collecting hundreds of computer drawings depicting children having their bodies sliced, mutilated, and displayed in disturbing and gory fashion.

I arrested Kimmo and he later pleaded to possession and distribution of child pornography. He is currently serving his time in federal prison. Was the suspect just drunk when he was chatting with PITH? Would he really "never harm a child" as he told us? Would he really have grabbed a kid from the mall and taken him to a cabin to be raped and tortured? We may never know for certain. I do know that for at least the next few years this guy will not have a chance to "make good" on his plans thanks to the hard work of the FBI, the U.S. Attorney's office, and our team of dedicated investigators.

File Sharing

Being able to communicate via the Internet has been a wonderful blessing to many. Such advances as the World Wide Web, email, and chat have made it easy to communicate with others around the globe. Another service that the Internet has provided us with is the ability to obtain files from other people and places. The ability to use the Internet to send files such as documents, photographs and audio and video files has been progressing to the point that it seems you can find almost anything through the Internet.

As people's desire to send and receive files have grown, so have the actual size of the files that people have sent and received. Movie files can grow to be very large in size and even with a fast Internet connection can take hours or days to transfer. As a result, several different methods of moving files via the Internet have evolved, including the concept of "file sharing". The concept of file sharing is simple in that it makes sending and receiving files, especially large files, faster by allowing multiple people with the same file to send and receive parts of the file to each other (thus distributing the workload over multiple internet connections and increasing the speed of file transfers). The first popular file sharing network was in 1999 when a program named Napster was created. Napster allowed people from around the world to share their music files with everyone else. Users searched Napster for a song that they wanted on the Napster computer servers and they could, in turn, download the audio file from dozens of people who had it on their computers. A song was simply a click away. The problem was that most all of the music was copyrighted and the distribution of the files for free was at the expense of someone else. Napster was forced to shut down its file sharing operations.

Over the years, new techniques and technologies have built upon the file sharing idea that Napster made so popular. Most

Internet File Sharing now occurs though "peer-to-peer" networks such as the Gnutella and BitTorrent protocols. These networks allow users from all over the world to trade everything from music to videos to software programs quickly and easily. These new networks and software do not have the limitations of having a single point of contact like Napster did; rather they allow the Internet to create a "hive" of file sharing computers which is difficult for copyright owners to track as they work like "peers" to each other. These peer-to-peer file sharing networks allow anyone access to millions of files from computers all around the world. Such files include not only music, photographs and documents, but also full length movies. As you can imagine this is a cause of concern for artists and others whose intellectual property is traded online as much of these files are copied illegally.

The file sharing networks are full of items that are inappropriate content for children. Also be aware that file sharing is not a one way process. This means that you are also actively sharing files from your computer to others on the Internet. If you download items that are illegal to possess, then you may also be responsible for simultaneously distributing those items. In addition, be aware that a large number of file sharing items available for download actually contain viruses and Trojan horse software that can severely affect the health of your computer and potentially compromise your computer and your personal security. Your children may find a treasure trove through file sharing…and you may find a costly virus and illegal content being shared on your behalf. Sharing of files is too risky for families and businesses to allow such activity on their computers. If you have, or if you find such programs as listed below, remove them, run and update your computer's anti-virus software and talk to your family about the dangers and legality of sharing files online.

Gnutella Network

The Gnutella Network can be accessed by any number of file sharing programs. The most popular file sharing program for the Gnutella network was LimeWire. LimeWire was shut down and forced to stop distributing the software via court injunction in 2010, however versions of LimeWire are still available online if one knows where to look. Other file sharing programs are still alive and well and are free online for download and installation. Some of the more popular Gnutella file sharing programs includes:

LimeWire

Frostwire

Bearshare

Phex

BitTorrent

The other very popular peer-to-peer file sharing network, BitTorrent works on a similar concept as Gnutella as each individual's computer shares bits, or portions of each file. They trade parts of a file that their computer has for other parts that they need in order to complete the entire file. BitTorrent has been around for over a decade and is one of the largest file sharing networks. There are dozens of programs that will allow you to trade files on the BitTorrent network. Some of the more popular BitTorrent clients include:

utorrent

Vuze (formally known as Azureus)

Bitcomet

Shareaza

Despite the fact that one can access nearly any type of document, photograph, movie or program with these types of programs there are some serious risks involved with downloading items via peer-to-peer networks. If you see these sorts of applications on your computer or other computers used by your children you need to be aware that these sorts of programs can allow them to access inappropriate and illegal material from the

Internet. If you find any of the above software or similar applications, remove them from all of your home computers. You may also need to check your anti-virus software and make sure that it is actively running and is updated. Many viruses and Trojan horse programs propagating on the file sharing networks disable anti-virus software on their victim's computers.

Newsgroups

Think of newsgroups as the Internet's version of the bulletin board down at your local grocery store. You know the ones, the big board that people in your neighborhood stick flyers on using tape or a push pin. They often say things like "lawn mowing services" and usually have a price and a phone number attached. You might see business cards and photos of homes in the area for sale also posted on the board. I always like to stop and see what flyers are advertising for sale. Newsgroups are just like the neighborhood bulletin board, except when you post a notice on an Internet newsgroup, people all over the world can read your posting and respond within seconds with a posting of their own. Newsgroups on the Internet aren't just limited to lawn mowing, real estate, and kittens however. You name the subject and there are newsgroups out there that will cater to your needs (more on that later). Newsgroups are also referred to as the Usenet. The information from the many different newsgroups was originally distributed via a wide-area network called the Usenet.

Newsgroups consist of various subjects and there are thousands of different groups available online. Newsgroups are hosted on various networks and servers around the globe. When information is posted to one particular newsgroup the posting is eventually shared with other servers that also host a particular newsgroup.

Connecting to the Newsgroups

Although you can obtain special newsgroup computer programs to access the multitude of newsgroups,

You also need to be aware that you should be quite proud of your posting as it may be around a lot longer than you are.

Newsgroup postings are being archived by Internet companies such as Google and may be around for a very long time.

If you are running an older Microsoft Operating System such as Windows XP your computer likely already has the ability to access newsgroups through the older versions of Microsoft's email program Outlook and Outlook Express. Windows Vista and Windows 7 do not have built in native newsgroup support. For that you will need to download a newsgroup reader application, or access web sites that archive and allow newsgroup access.

Once connected with a Newsgroup reader program you will want to download the list of the available newsgroup subjects. This may take a while with some 50,000 to 100,000 or more newsgroup names that need to be downloaded to your computer.

As you will find, there are newsgroups for every kind of subject matter and activity. Newsgroup postings originally only contained text; however, as newsgroups evolved they soon began to add photographs, sounds, and even movies to the posted messages in the form of "binary" files. It doesn't take long to figure out that the most popular newsgroups on the Internet are the ones that contain adult pornography. Newsgroups like the famous alt.sex postings contain tens of thousands of adult pornography (including photos and movies). There are many newsgroups that contain many explicit, deviant, and in some cases, illegal sexual practices such as:

> alt.binaries.beastiality
> alt.binaries.pictures.eroctica.rape
> alt.sex.pedophile

Not exactly the kinds of things you want your children (at any age) exposed to. There is even newsgroup software that when properly setup will go out to your favorite pornography newsgroup and automatically download all of the photographs that are contained therein. I first learned about these programs from a child sexual predator who was using a newsgroup reading program called "Binary Boy" to download hundreds of child pornography images. Within a couple of hours one can amass thousands of photographs from hundreds of different newsgroups without even breaking a sweat. Did I fail to mention that newsgroups and all of the items contained therein are completely free? That's right. All of the text, photographs and movies on the Newsgroups are all free to anyone with a computer, an Internet connection, some knowledge, and a little time on their hands.

One free newsgroup application for Windows, Agent from Forte (www.forteinc.com) allows access to newsgroup servers. They even have a 30 day free trial version for download. Below I used Agent to access a newsgroup server. I asked for a directory of the groups available. It returned over 100,000 different newsgroups (Figure 10).

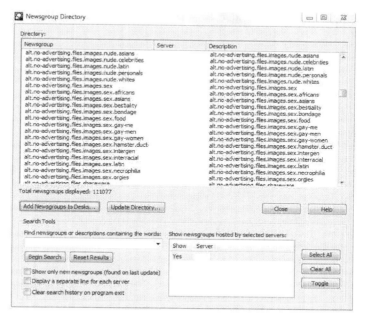

Figure 10

In less than five minutes, I had free access to any of the above 100,000 different newsgroups; including many with pornography and illegal content, all filled with free content to download.

Cell Phones

The rapid expansion of the use of cellular telephones has taken the concerns of parents and law enforcement to new heights. As the concerns over the use of computers by our children in our homes has continued, the advent of cell phones means that the reach of the Internet now extends well beyond just your home. The problem of course is that your children and their cell phones now have full internet access 24 hours a day, 7 days a week anywhere and everywhere they go. They have a fully functional computer in their pocket and many have access to high speed internet access no matter where they are. That means that all of the internet concerns that I talked about above, such as the world wide web, email, chat, social networking, and now text and video mean that our children are able to access people and people can access them even more easily, anytime, anywhere.

The addition of high quality cameras in cell phones and video capture also means that the phone/computer in their pocket allows for more potential problems and concerns for families. Parents need to be aware of the power of cellular telephones; everything that we are about to discuss in the way of protecting your children and your family applies to the use of cellular telephones.

Today cellular texting and chat messaging for kids, especially teenagers, has become the preferred method in which they like to communicate with each other and with the world. Many of us know the experience of having your teenager with their heads in their cell phone and their thumbs on the keyboard typing away another message to their "BFF" (Best Friend Forever). Our kids have developed their own method and language for texting and chatting. I spend hours decoding their often encrypted like short hand and abbreviation. It is often difficult to keep up with their ongoing lingo.

Texting/Chatting shorthand often looks like this:

53X   means "Sex"
STBY means "Sucks To Be You"
P911 means "Parent Alert"
KPC   means "Keeping Parents Clueless"

There are thousands of different acronyms, symbols, and other codes that your kids use. If you need more assistance in decrypting your children's text and chat messages one very good online resource is www.netlingo.com (see Figure 11).

HOME   DICTIONARY   BY CATEGORY   WORD OF THE DAY   ADD/EDIT

Figure 11

Netlingo.com has lots of up-to-date text and messaging information that can assist you in breaking your kid's online messages and "codes".

Your child as a victim

In this chapter I will tell you how to help protect your child from becoming a victim of the Internet. I will tell you more about what you have to fear from the World Wide Web, the chat rooms, email, Internet stalkers, cyber-harassment, and potential loss of privacy. I will also give you advice and my suggestions for how to do battle against each of these threats leveled at you and your children. Before we begin I want to stop and take a moment to give you the number one thing that all parents should do to begin keeping their children safe from the dangers on the Internet. Now listen closely as I'm only going to repeat this about ten more times throughout this book. You can do EVERYTHING that I suggest in this book, but if you fail to do this one thing you will most likely lose nearly all of the benefits that you have made in protecting your child while online. The one thing that you should do is this simple step:

Get the Internet out of your child's bedroom (that includes their cell phone).

This idea is based upon the many observations I have made during hundreds of investigations and search warrants in the homes of victims and suspects involving the Internet. A child with a computer or a cell phone and unfiltered or unmonitored Internet access is a constant factor in nearly all of the computer crime cases I have seen in my career. Whenever I go to the home of a juvenile suspect or victim, I nearly always find that the child has had unlimited access to the Internet and that the access is in their bedroom or on their cell phone.

Your children should not have free reign to go and see

everything on the Internet that they want to. This is worse than giving them the keys to the candy store. The worst thing that will come from full access to the candy aisle is a tummy ache. On the Internet, however, your child can victimize and be victimized without even realizing it until it is too late to take back that mouse click. Your children need guidance and like it or not, it is your job to provide that guidance. I am willing to give you the tools to help guide them along their journey on the Internet. That being said, as the parent and the adult, you need to make sure that your kids have some restraints placed upon them. Putting a fully operational computer and full Internet access in their bedroom places them in greater danger and more risk of harm.

In the following chapters I am going to tell you about many of the potential trouble spots along the roads of the Internet and give you some advice and guidance along the way.

From the CyberCop case files:
The Babysitter Molesters

Bert and his girlfriend had a deal. She would continue to provide him with one of the little girls that she babysat and he would continue to be her boyfriend. By giving him a child to molest, he would be Cara's man. Cara knew that Bert had a past. She knew that he had been to prison for the sexual assault of a child. She knew that Bert was a child predator. She would do anything for him; even harm a child that she was entrusted to protect.

Bert and Cara had been sending emails and chatting with each other for years. They had been friends before Bert went to prison back in the 1980s. Bert was an extremely intelligent and highly educated man. He was even a high school teacher at one time. He was also a lifelong child molester.

We first received word that something was wrong when Bert's victim was brought into the hospital. She was only 8 years old. She had been acting out sexually and was complaining of pains "down there." Her grandmother was concerned and told us that the victim spent a great deal of time with her babysitter Cara and her boyfriend, Bert. We did some looking into Bert's background and quickly discovered that Bert not only had a history of child molestation, he was currently on probation and was not supposed to have any contact with kids. We learned this from a check of our statewide sexual offender database located on the Internet (www.dps.state.ak.us/nSorcr/asp/). If your state does not have an online sexual offender database, I highly recommend that you look into what it would take to get one created. I also learned that Bert was trained in computers, something he had developed proficiency in during his prison stay.

The interview with the victim told the story. She told the interviewer that she would go over to her babysitter's apartment. When Bert was there he would touch her and make her touch him. As this 8 year old girl spoke of the many different sexual positions and activities that Bert and Cara engaged her in, it became difficult for me to watch. She talked about Bert using a camera and using a computer to take pictures with "no clothes on." She was an extremely articulate and honest victim. She was able to tell investigators things that clearly identified her babysitter and Bert as the perpetrators. A physical examination by a staff of clinicians confirmed the girl's story. We began immediately to draft up search warrants for the homes of Bert and Cara.

I headed up the team of investigators directed to execute the search of Bert's house. At the residence we found Bert and quickly placed him into handcuffs. He was immediately arrested for violating his conditions of probation. In the house we found a computer network along with a scanner and various storage media (disks, CDs, DVDs).

Bert agreed to speak with interviewers and denied any wrongdoing. He stated that he did not know our victim and didn't even know who she was. One of the interviewers asked me if I had any questions for Bert. I walked over to Bert and asked him a simple question. "Do you have any security or passwords that I need to be aware of before I begin examining your computer?" Bert looked at me with a smug look on his face and grunted "I don't know!" I asked him "What am I going to find on your computer? Is there anything that you want to tell me now?" Bert shrugged his shoulders and said nothing. I threw up my hands, turned and began walked back into the house to finish packing up the computers. Some cases of child sexual assault will rest on the testimony of the victim's word versus the word of the suspect. If there is little or no physical evidence some cases may come down to "he said, she said." I was determined to find some evidence to prevent that from happening.

I quickly discovered that Bert was not being honest with us. His computer hard drive information had been password protected. He did not want anyone to see what was on his computer. After several days I was able to disable his password and examine the data which explained why he did not want anyone to gain access. On the computer's hard drive I discovered hundreds of child pornography images. It appeared that Bert had been obtaining child pornography from the Internet, most likely from the Internet Newsgroups (see the chapter entitled, "What are Newsgroups").

I also located email messages between Bert and Cara. In the messages they used a semi-coded style of typing; however it soon became apparent that the two of them were planning out their sexual meetings with our victim. Later they would use the Internet to email each other about what he wanted to do with her sexually the next time they were together. They discussed what they could do for the victim for being such a "good girl."

This was really good evidence. This was the kind

of thing that makes cases and puts the bad guys away in prison. I still was not satisfied. I had to find the images of the victim. I was sure that she was correct when she said that Bert took photos of her using a Polaroid type camera. She called it a "camera where the picture comes out of it." I looked and found more child pornography. I even found some child porn that Bert had encrypted, but I still could not find what we were looking for. I recalled that Bert had a scanner attached to his computer when we came through the door of his residence. Could that be the key? If Bert did take still photographs of the victim, he must have used his scanner to get them into the computer. I looked in the area of the computer where the scanner software was located. I know that computer software will often default to the directory (or folder) that it resides in. If a person fails to tell the software where exactly to save and image, or doesn't pay attention to the name of the folder, the software will often save the image in the folder that it resides in. Often people will save their documents and photographs inside of computer folders like "My Documents" or "My Photos". One can check the computer application folders for documents that were accidentally saved inside. It was when I looked inside of the scanner folder that I found it. There I located a file that Bert had not meant to save. I found what appeared to be a test or a preview scan of a single Polaroid type photograph. The picture was mistakenly placed upside down on the scanner and had most likely been a first attempt at getting a proper scan. I selected the image, rotated it so that it was right side up, and electronically zoomed in.

What I found was a photograph of our victim, completely nude and spread out on a bed. You could clearly make out our victim's face, the bed, the bedding, etc.. Upon comparison of the babysitter's bed and setting there was a perfect match. We had what we needed to make this an open and shut case. What we did not have, were the other untold number of Polaroid-type pictures and computer images that Bert and Cara had no doubt taken. We never located the other photographs and despite my best efforts I never found another computer image of our victim. To this day I do not know what the suspects did with them, or where they are located. Are they stashed away in some wall, or buried in some corner of the property? And are they out on the Internet being traded and distributed by other Internet Predators who are coveting them even as you read this? I wish I knew the answer.

World Wide Web & Your Kids

The World Wide Web (WWW) allows you and your kid's access to over a trillion (as in 1,000,000,000,000) web pages from around the world. Your child can go to the Library of Congress (www.loc.gov) and do research on virtually every topic that they can think of. They can travel to countries around the world or learn about life, science (www.scientificamerican.com) or anything else that they want to know. They also can go to web sites and learn about how to make pipe bombs, how to make alcohol, and how to hate. They can not only access the normal "run-of-the-mill adult pornography but they can also obtain graphic images of every sexually deviant act that can be thought of (most of which I had never heard of until I became a cop). In many of these cases the web information, the pictures, and the videos on the Internet are often free of charge while others are not. That often explains why I have had lots of cases on my desk where kids have stolen their parent's credit card and have used it to gain access to pay per web sites.

Pornography

Gone are the days when the only place that kids could get pornography was from their best friend's dad's sock drawer or from under their big brother's bed. Growing up, the only place that I had even a remote possibility of getting adult pornography was behind the counter at the local liquor store. Even then you had to be over 21 and have a valid driver's license.

Spend less than five minutes online today and you will see that your kids have access to pornography like no generation before them. The porn industry is alive and well online and has been on the Net for years. Surprisingly the adult porn industry has been the innovators when it comes to the Internet and web commerce. Adult web pioneered the successful use of online credit card transactions (and made use of some of the first secure/encrypted transactions as well). They were one of the first to use live streaming audio and video systems. The adult web sites are the one business on the Internet that consistently makes money and is estimated to take in over a billion dollars a year. They are online and they do not appear to be going away anytime soon. Recently the domain extension of .xxx (as instead of .com) became available in an attempt to put adult web sites in their own "red light district" of the internet. Although .xxx domains are now available there is no requirement to have any of the of the millions of adult .com web sites move to .xxx so this will have little impact on Internet porn access for your kids

One of the clear problems with adult pornography online is that when your child inadvertently or actively accesses adult materials they are continually exposed to images that degrade woman and creates an unhealthy view of relationships. I don't see many people asking what the effects are on our children when they are exposed to this large and unfiltered amount of pornography. What happens to a young man who is just beginning to develop sexually and who has uncontrolled access to hundreds of thousands of images of adult pornography? What are his expectations of the other sex? What about young and developing girls who are exposed to adult pornography? How does that affect their self-esteem and their future relationships? These are hard questions to answer. Here are some even more difficult questions for parents to ask:

> What happens to the child who is exposed to online images of sexual masochistic acts (bondage/torture)?

> How about images from the web of women being raped?

Do you think that photographs of bodies taken during an autopsy would affect a child?

What about gruesome photos from an actual crime scene?

What about a teenager whom I located and who had downloaded thousands of images of children engaged in sexual acts?

These are actual situations and real images found in the possession of our children during cases that I have investigated. I don't think anyone has an easy answer to these kinds of tough child-developmental questions. I believe that the answer lies in preventing your child from being exposed to this sort of material in the first place, rather than having to deal with the consequences at some later date.

Hate Sites

The Internet has created a perfect place for people who think they know best and want everyone else to know how they think. I'm talking about the white supremacist groups, the neo-Nazis, the Skinheads, the Ku Klux Klan, al-Queda, and the Aryan Nations or anyone else with a computer, an Internet connection, and a dislike for people other than themselves. The Internet allows people like this to spread their message of racist garbage, to gather intelligence about their enemies, to exchange information among themselves, and to recruit new members. It's cheap and easy for them to use the Internet to maintain their presence online. Using Internet search engines (Google, Bing, Yahoo, Ask.com, etc.) you can find web sites that proclaim hate for just about everything and everyone. The al-Qaeda terrorist group are a particular hate group who has leveraged the Internet in very sophisticated and efficient ways to spread their hate of the West.

Besides hating someone or something these sites have other things in common. They use fear, misinformation, historical revisionism, spiritual or religious references, and even patriotism as ways to justify their racist platforms.

I once learned of a very successful local white supremacist organization in my area that had created a sophisticated Internet web site which allows other white supremacists from around the world to create their own hate web sites. At last count they had over 100 different hate sites up and running. They provide this service for free and are running it right here in my own hometown. As parents we have to realize that this sort of thing is out on the Internet and it does not matter if the web site is located on the other side of the world or across town. Borders are meaningless as their messages of hate and intolerance know no bounds. As a police officer and a parent I find hate to be an unacceptable message to send to our kids (even if it is covered by free speech).

Anarchists/Bomb recipes

How quickly can your kids locate directions for making high explosives and bombs? It took me about sixty seconds to search the Internet using search engines and personal web pages to find over 200 different recipes for everything from how to make exploding light bulbs to manufacturing the explosive Nitroglycerine. It wasn't difficult. In fact, I found that it was way too easy for anyone at any age to get this information (Figure 12).

The information itself is not usually illegal to possess (check your local laws). However, it is what a person does with the information that is of concern. If your child is downloading these recipes all in the spirit of "learning" or "education," at what point does he or she decide to actually try these out to see if they really work? Kids are by nature curious creatures. Remember how curious we were as children? Curiosity coupled with easy to get recipes for making pipe bombs can be a deadly combination.

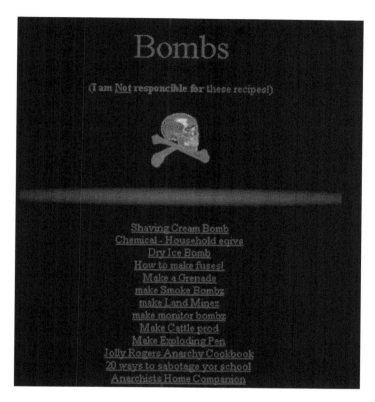

Figure 12

Parents need to be aware that many of these bomb "recipes" are often inaccurate. I have had some of my explosives expert colleagues review some online bomb instructions and they tell me that some of these recipes have been altered or written in such a way as to actually cause the bomb or the ingredients to explode in the hands of anyone who tries to build some of these devices.

What Parents can do about the World Wide Web (WWW)

How do you prevent your child from inadvertently (or on purpose) seeing pornography, hate groups, anarchists/bombs, and drugs on the Internet? One way is to get the Internet Access and online devices out of their bedrooms (or other unsupervised areas) and into a place where you can monitor what your kids are doing.

Some the other avenues for safe web surfing includes:

1) Sit down and devote time to use the World Wide Web with your children. That way you can discuss what web sites you are going to go to and you can be there to help direct their interests. By being part of the experience you can help answer questions and give guidance.

2) Set up Internet and web-surfing rules for your child to follow. Let them know what appropriate material is and what appropriate web sites are. They also need to know about your rules of what web sites and material are not acceptable. Before your child breaks a rule they need to know what the consequences will be and you need to follow through. If your child breaks the rules, then they need to know why they are being sanctioned.

3) Take the time to visit web sites that have been deemed child or kid friendly. It's the old idea of "try before you buy." Visit sites so that you can judge for yourself what is appropriate material for your kids and your teens. There are many good sites available, but you really need to take the time to check them out. I suggest that you start with sites such as these:

www.ala.org and gws.ala.org
www.ipl.org
www.getnetwise.org

www.kidsinmind.com (this web site is a good one for parents to check movies for appropriateness before taking your kids to the movies).

4)   Check up on your child's web surfing activities from time to time. Ask them what sites they like and don't like. Also you may want to consider making a habit of walking by the child while they are on the computer every few minutes. In some cases there may be a time when you feel that it is necessary to search the computer outside of your child's presence to see where they have been on the web (see the next section: Checking your child's web activities).

Checking Your Child's Web Activities

You can and should check up on your child's Internet activities from time to time. You do not have to spend money for some complex computer software designed to track their web surfing although there is software out there that will do it. It is a parental right and responsibility to see that your children are following the rules. One parent I spoke with was concerned about her daughter using the computer during after school hours when she wasn't yet home from work. Her daughter had constantly disobeyed the rules regarding the computer and the Internet. She finally came up with a temporary solution by taking the keyboard to work with her every day. When she returned from work she reattached the keyboard and then was able to monitor her daughter's Internet activity. I was taken with the woman's simple and inexpensive solution to her concern. Hopefully, you will never be in that kind of situation, however it does pay to be creative in finding ways to keep your child safe on the Internet.

Web Caches and Web Histories

The first thing you have to decide is which web browsing software do you and your kids use? In the majority of cases it will be either Microsoft's Internet Explorer or Mozilla Firefox or in some cases you may have both programs on your computer (see the chapter entitled "What is... the World Wide Web" for these and other web browsing applications).

When a person uses these types of applications to go to different web sites both of these web browsers will often save pieces of their web surfing activities on your computer's hard disk drive. On a Windows based personal computer the main hard disk drive is referred to as the "C" or "C:" drive.

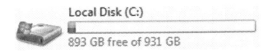

Local Disk (C:)

893 GB free of 931 GB

The web browsers save web surfing information which includes the name of the web sites, the web site's text and even the graphics. When you go to a web site such as www.nick.com, the web browser asks for and receives all of the web page information including text, colors, images, animation and everything that you see on the web page. That information is then temporarily stored on your computer hard disk drive. Should you need to go back to a particular web site that you were recently at the web browser checks to see if portions of the web site are still located on your hard disk drive. That way the web browser does not have to bother with downloading the entire site again. The area of your computer that contains old web site information is often referred to as the "cache." We can use this old web information to our advantage.

In this example I am using Internet Explorer version 9 running on the Windows 7. Other versions of Windows (Windows Vista, XP, ect.) may be slightly different than the examples shown below.

To determine what types of web sites your children are going to when they are using Internet Explorer open up the Internet Explorer application.

Internet Explorer

In the upper right hand corner of the Internet Explorer web program there are three symbols, a house ⌂, a star ★, and a gear ⚙ (Figure 13).

Figure 13

Click on the star symbol ⭐ (Figure 14).

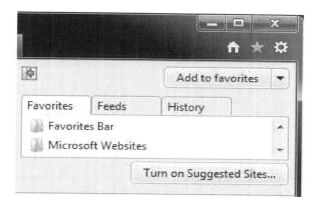

Figure 14

Click on the tab marked "History". This will display the history for the browser's web site usage by date, such as the past several days or week (Figure 15).

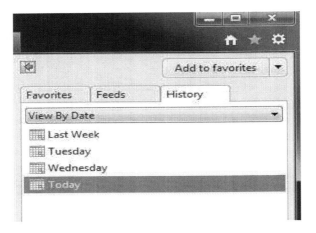

Figure 15

By clicking the calendar for "Today" you can see the webs sites and places that I visited in during this particular day (Figure 16).

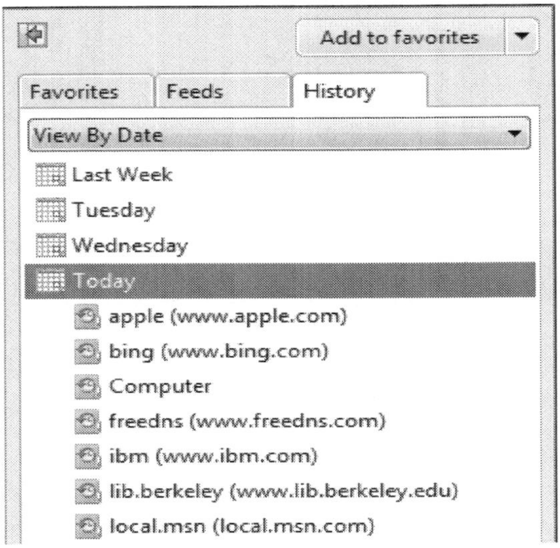

Figure 16

As you can see I went to several web sites during the day, including a web site for IBM (IBM.com). By clicking on the pull down tab that says "View By Date" you can select other options to view the Internet History (Figure 17). You can then look at other web visits in several ways including by "most visited". In this way you can get more information about web surfing trends on the computer.

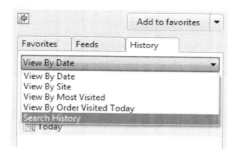

Figure 17

What if the Internet Explorer History list is empty? What then? The first thing to do is to realize that the History folder is not normally empty. The History folder begins to fill up and items are deleted over time by the web browser. There is a way to clean out the web browsing history.

Internet Explorer allows for emptying of the web history by clicking on the gear icon in the upper right hand corner of Explorer. Scroll down and click on "Internet Options" (Figure 18).

Figure 18

On the first page of the "Internet Options" you will see a section for "Browser History. A person can click on the "Delete..." button and clear out the history of the web browser. You can also check the option box to "Delete browser history on exit" (Figure 19). This will hide your web surfing by automatically deleting all of your web activities when you quit Internet Explorer.

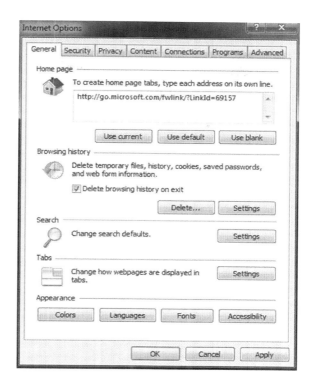

Figure 19

Microsoft Internet Explorer 9 also has a built in option called "InPrivate" browsing which allows web surfing during a session where no history, temporary files, or other data is kept. The other major web applications, Mozilla Firefox and Google's Chrome web browser also have similar anonymous browsing settings.

With all of that being said if the history folder is empty and you are certain that you or someone else has been on the computer to web surf using Internet explorer then the fact that the web history is empty is a clue that someone may be trying to hide their Internet tracks. You need to wonder who is hiding their web activity and why they might want to do so.

C is for Cookie

In terms of web surfing on the Internet, "cookies" are little bits of data that are left in your computer as you visit different web sites (they are not chocolate chips). The main reason for web sites to leave these cookies is to track such non-threatening things as "the last time visited," "which areas on their site you visited" or "which web browser do you use." This information can be helpful to the web site in helping to make your visiting their web site more enjoyable and efficient.

I like to use the cookie information left on a computer to add to my mountain of evidence while investigating a person's computer. Even if the person has deleted the items in the web browser's cache (the HTML files and photos, etc.) I can still get a pretty good picture of the kinds of places that the person goes to and likes to "hang out" in by looking for left over cookie files.

In Windows 7, Internet Explorer keeps its list of cookies and cookie files in a hidden folder located on your computer's hard disk drive located at:

C:\Users\UserName\AppData\Roaming\Microsoft\Windows\Cookies

The "Username" is the user account for a particular person, in my case the Internet cookie files are in:

C:\Users\Glen\AppData\Roaming\Microsoft\Windows\Cookies

Be aware that the folder is usually hidden and there are options in Windows to show hidden files and folders.

One easy way to pull up the cookie folder in Windows 7 is to go to the Start/Search button located in the lower left hand corner of the Windows Desktop. Click on it and in the search box enter "shell:cookies" (Figure 20).

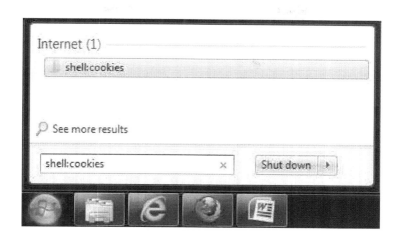

Figure 20

Each file in the Cookies folder represents a cookie file left by a web site (Figure 21). Inside of the cookie file may be a specific web site that left the cookie file. The information is usually only readable by the web site that created it and is designed to help you in recalling where you were on a web site, your preferences, settings, or other features specific to that web site.

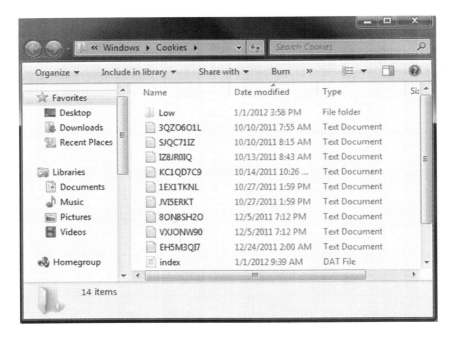

Figure 21

Using an editing program such as Notepad/WordPad or even Microsoft Word you can open up and view the cookie files one at a time.

Here, I opened up one cookie file which appears to show some data from a music playing web site I often visit called Pandora.com (Figure 22).

Figure 22

Looking through your cookie files does not give you a complete picture of where your family is web surfing, but it may help give you some valuable data in which to make some good decisions.

Cookies have gotten a bad reputation over the years, as some paranoid types believe that cookies were another way for someone to be able to track you and your web browsing activities. That is only partially true. In a small number of cases, cookie files have been used by other people to gain some small bits of information about people's data. If you monitor your web usage and use and update your anti-virus regularly the likelihood of you losing critical personal information is really quite low.

If you are worried about cookies (and believe me there are bigger threats to you out on the Internet than cookies), then I suggest turning off the feature in your web browser that allows cookies to be placed on your hard drive.

To turn off the Internet Explorer cookies functions, go back to your Internet Explorer program and open up the gear icon ⚙ located in the upper right hand corner of the program.

Select the option that says "Internet Options" (Figure 23).

Figure 23

Click on the tab that says "Privacy" and then click on the button that says "Advanced" (
Figure 24).

Figure 24

Check the box that says "Override automatic cookie handling" and change the two Cookie settings to read "Block" (Figure 25).

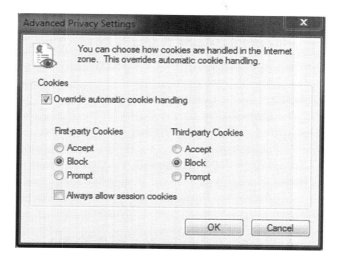

Figure 25

Click on the OK button and your Internet Explorer 9 will no longer accept cookies from other web sites. Be aware that turning off your web cookies may affect your web surfing experience and that some legitimate sites that you want to visit may require that cookies be turned on to allow full access.

Internet Filtering and Tracking Software

One method of trying to keep Internet kids safe has been the popular use of computer software programs to filter and track your children while they are on the Internet. The idea is not a bad one however as we shall see these programs cannot completely protect your kids while they are online. These programs often tend to give parents a false sense of security when in reality they may not be working at all.

Internet Filters

Please allow me to take a moment to tell you why I believe that Internet filters do not always work. When they do work they can block out so many sites that families become frustrated and will sometimes end up turning them completely off. Parents who spend their money on these kinds of programs often believe that they are keeping their children completely safe. There is no magic pill or technological babysitter that will protect your kids from Internet harm. With that being said, let us take a look at the different types of Internet filters and see how you can use them.

Search Engine Filters

A search engine such as Google (www.google.com) or Bing (www.bing.com) are web sites that take your request for information and comb through the billions of web sites and attempt to provide you with the information that you requested. By entering a key word or phrase, the search engine will list a series of web sites that closely match what it was that you were looking for. Sometimes you get what you want, and sometimes you don't.

Search engines are notorious for presenting the user with a large amount of options, many of which are inappropriate for children. For example, doing research on breast cancer can sometimes return items that are extremely pornographic in nature.

I recall one telephone message that I received from a lady who was on the web looking for a Fireweed Jelly recipes (which tastes very good by the way). After entering the phrase "fireweed" and "recipe" into an Internet search engine, she received a series of possible sites that matched. When she clicked on one of the sites she was shown a photograph of a very young female girl wearing no clothes. The young girl was holding a bouquet of fireweed flowers in her hand.

There are some Internet search engines that try to be more suited for family web searches. These search engines are designed to not allow most of the inappropriate material in their databases to be returned back to you during a search. The search engine Google (www.google.com) is one. It has billions of web sites in its database and is free to use. I also like the fact that it isn't all cluttered up with annoying advertising displays. Google provides a way to filter some of the search results that are returned to you using their SafeSearch function. Google clearly states that no search filtering is 100% accurate (which is true) and that using filtered searches may also filter out other items that you are actually looking for (which is also true). Of course, in order to filter the items that Google returns during a search you first have to turn on the filter option. A note of caution, if you decided to turn off your cookies in the prior chapter (C is for Cookie), you may need to turn them back on for Google SafeSearch to work.

To set up Google's SafeSearch capabilities, go to their web site at www.google.com/preferences. Select the SafeSearch Filters and move the toggle box from "Moderate" to "Strict" (Figure 26).

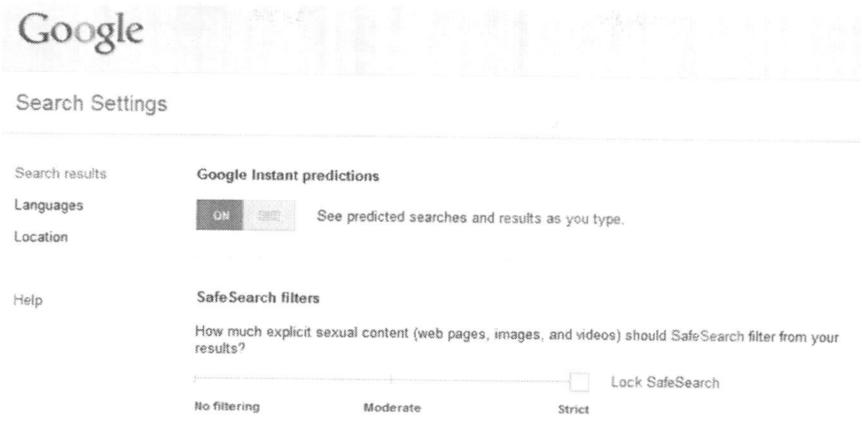

Figure 26

Scroll down the page and click on the "Save" button to keep your new setting.

The next time that you use Google to search the World Wide Web, Google will attempt to filter out the adult web sites and other inappropriate material. Please be aware that no filter system can eliminate all material from young eyes, however, according to my experience Google does do a good job of stopping most filtered material from being displayed on your computer. Google still allows searches for words that may be appropriate in some instances. As in the example that is used above, if you or your child is working on a report about breast cancer research, searching with Google's SafeSearch set to "Strict" will accept the term "breast cancer" and it returns sites that are appropriate to the research.

Microsoft's Search engine Bing.com (www.bing.com) also provides content filtering. To activate content filtering in Bing, go to www.bing.com and click on their preferences icon, a gear icon

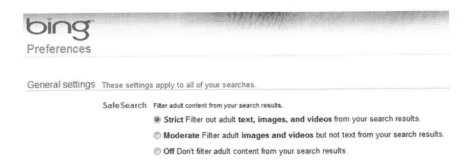, in the upper right hand corner of the web page.

The Bing preference web page will appear (Figure 27).

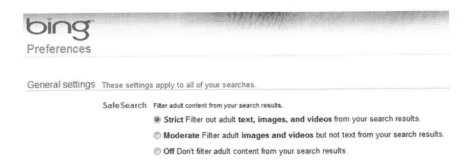

Figure 27

Set the amount of filtering that you want and then locate the "Save" button on the page and click on it to save your selection.

Another popular web search engine Ask (www.ask.com) has a separate search engine specifically designed for kids ages 6-12 years old. It can be accessed online at: www.askkids.com.

Internet Content Filters at Home

Setting preferences is great for a search engine, but what about other more specific filtering of your Internet? There are dozens of products currently on the market that promise to protect your child from the evils of the Internet. Some of the more popular filtering software programs include Bsecure (http://www.bsecure.com), Cyber Patrol (www.cyberpatrol.com), CyberSitter (www.cybersitter.com), and Net Nanny (www.netnanny.com). These programs sell for less than $100 and several of them are now including filtering of cellular telephone internet data as well.

The question that I am most often asked about these programs is, "Do they work?" The answer is that they do indeed work in many cases and they can be very helpful in filtering your family's online activities; however, they do not completely solve all of the Internet problems faced by most families. They are not 100% accurate in blocking out all unwanted web content, email, chat rooms or newsgroups and will often block out some sites that are legitimate for children to see. Some of these programs can perform Internet tracking of where your child goes while they are on the Internet. These programs often use lists of questionable web sites or key words as the basis for blocking or allowing certain sites to be used. These lists need to be updated regularly in order to be effective. Some computer techies have managed to figure out a way to find the actual "banned" web locations from some of the filtered software secret lists. The filtered lists have been making the rounds of the Internet and the local high schools. Internet perverts have also gathered the filtered lists and have been accessing the web sites on these "banned" lists for their own gratification.

Parents also need to be aware that there are web sites out on the Internet that will help teach your kids how to bypass many of the filtering software programs. People online offer programs that detect Internet Filtering and tracking software and teach kids how to disengage the filters or reveal the parental passwords.

If you choose to use such applications don't ever stop being vigilant and involved in keeping your kids safe on the Internet. Internet filtering software such as those listed above can be used and they can be effective, however, no filtering software in the world can replace an actively engaged and present parent when it comes to safety.

Microsoft's Family Safety

The Windows 7 Operating System comes with many very cool features built into it and one of the new and improved set of features it has is designed to help make your family safer while on the Internet. The system is called Windows Live Family Safety and is made of up several parts. The Microsoft Live Family Safety system provides a multitude of features including:

> Setting computer use time limits
> Limiting the types of games your kids can play
> Restricting certain computer programs
> Blocking of downloads
> Limiting who can contact your children online
> Filtering explicit online content

The Windows Live Family Safety has three parts to it. The first part is the Family Safety Filter which can be installed on each of your Windows 7 computers and will monitor your kid's computer use. The second part of the Family Safety is the Windows Parental Controls which allow you to set specific safety settings for your kids computer use. The third part is a Family Safety website that ties together all of the computers that you have Family Safety filters on them and allows you to monitor and maintain them.

Installing Family Safety

Microsoft's Family Safety requires that you have an account (or ID) on the Microsoft Live web servers. A Windows Live ID is an account that you create to access such services as Microsoft Hotmail or Microsoft Xbox Live. Assuming that you don't have a Windows Live ID account you will need to create one. To set up a Windows Live account, go to the web site at:

signup.live.com

You will be asked to provide some basic information such as your name, email address and the like (Figure 28). Not everyone in your family needs one. You only need to setup one Windows Live ID account for yourself.

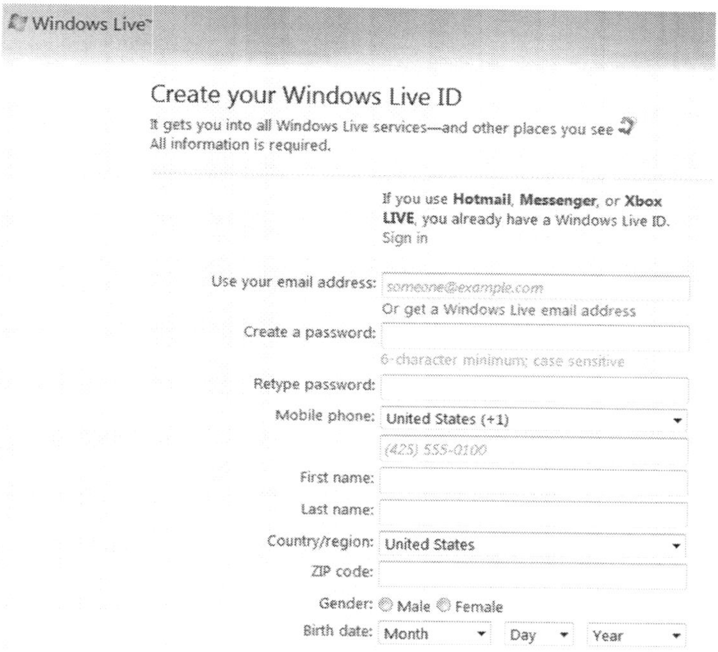

Figure 28

Enter the required information and click the "Accept" button near the bottom of the page. Normally an email will be set to the email address that you entered for verification. You will need to check your email for a message from Microsoft Live and follow the directions in order to activate your Microsoft Live account.

Once you have a Windows Live account you need to check and see if your Windows 7 computer has the Windows Live Family

Safety Software installed.

Click on the Start/Search Button 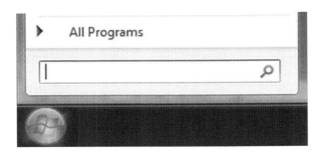 in the lower left hand corner of your Windows Desktop. Click on the "All Programs" bar (Figure 29).

Figure 29

Look for a folder entitled "Windows Live" (Figure 30).

Figure 30

If you don't have it installed you will need to download and install the Windows Live Essentials software which includes the Family Safety Software. It can be downloaded from Microsoft here:

http://go.microsoft.com/fwlink/?LinkId=136325

Download and install the Windows Live Essentials software onto your computer (Figure 31).

Figure 31

Once installed go back to the Start/Search Button in the lower left hand corner of your Windows Desktop. Click on the "All Programs" bar and click on the Windows Live Family Safety program (Figure 32).

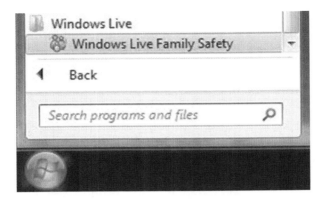

Figure 32

The first time you run the Family Safety Program it will ask that you log into Windows Live. Log in using your email and Windows Live password that you created earlier (Figure 33).

Figure 33

Once you are signed in, the Family Safety Application searches the computer that you are currently using for all of the user accounts that are present. Many people don't even know that your Windows computer can and should have user accounts for each person who uses the computer. Most people setup one account with their computer and everyone uses that same login account. If you and your family fall into that category I suggest that you start by setting up an account for each person on every computer used by each family member. In the long run it makes managing your computers easier, and doing so allows each person to customize their own desktop, applications, photos, etc. It also allows Microsoft's Family Safety to track each person and setup different things for different people in the house. In this case I am using our family computer located in the family room. The computer is named "Familyroom-PC". On our Family computer I have three user accounts. There is one for myself and one for each of the boys, Jay and Evan. If, like most people you only setup one main user on your computer you will need to create a Windows account for each person that will be using this particular computer that you are on. You can click on the sentence that says "create a new standard Windows Account" to create an account for each of your family members.

Once installed, Windows Live Family Safety sees all of our user accounts including my administrator account. Administrator accounts allow you to have complete access and control over the entire computer, including all of the users. That is why you don't want to give your kids administrator rights. Make their account standard Windows accounts.

The first time you open up Windows Live family Safety it will assist you in setting up the accounts (Figure 34).

Figure 34

If you already have set up user accounts then you will be shown a list of existing accounts. If you haven't yet set up accounts, have no fears you can create new accounts here as well (Figure 35).

Figure 35

Simply check the accounts that you wish to monitor (Figure 36).

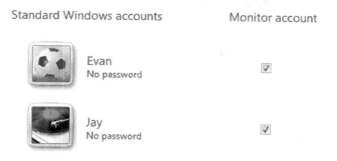

Figure 36

Click on the "next" button to continue.

Once Family Safety knows which users to manage it will show you the current user accounts that you have told it to monitor. Below you can see that both Evan and Jay's user accounts on this Family room computer is set to filter out adult web sites and that their computer activity will be reported back to you via your Windows Live ID account (Figure 37).

Figure 37

To check your work you can go into your Microsoft Live Family Safety website by going to:

Familysafety.live.com

Once logged in, you can manage and see reports generated by the users that you are monitoring and filtering (Figure 38).

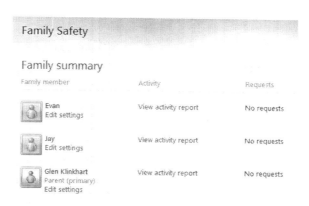

Figure 38

Going into the user settings you can adjust various items for each person. For example, you can adjust their web filtering, time limits, activity reporting, game restrictions, and program restrictions (Figure 39).

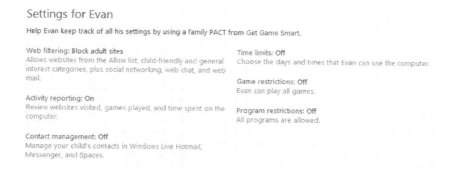

Figure 39

With time restrictions, you can set when each user can use the computer, even for weekends. Below, I set restrictions to Evan's account so that he cannot use the computer from 9pm through 3pm Monday through Friday but he can stay up and use the computer until 10pm on Friday and Saturday (Figure 40).

Select times when Evan can use the computer

◉ Turn on time limits   ○ Turn off time limits (Activity reports will still be provided)

Select the hours you want to allow. ☐ Allowed ▮▮▮▮ Blocked

	Sun	Mon	Tue	Wed	Thu	Fri	Sat
12 AM							
1 AM							
2 AM							
3 AM							
4 AM							
5 AM							
6 AM							
7 AM							
8 AM							
9 AM							
10 AM							
11 AM							
12 PM							
1 PM							
2 PM							
3 PM							
4 PM							
5 PM							
6 PM							
7 PM							
8 PM							
9 PM							
10 PM							
11 PM							

Figure 40

If your child tries to login or use the computer after the block time, Windows won't allow them to login or will log them off if they are on the account.

With online web filtering activated, a user who attempts to access inappropriate content such as adult web sites will be greeted with the following message (Figure 41):

This page is blocked

http://www.playboy.com/

Ask your parent for permission to view this page

Email your request

Ask in person

Check out other websites

See a list of child-friendly websites

Figure 41

And you will be notified in the reporting feature of your Windows Family Safety Web account.

The Windows Live Family Safety system has a lot of options and you must be willing to be committed to setting it up and monitoring it. I won't say that it is easy; you will need to do a lot of work on the front end. Don't forget that you will need to install Windows Live Family Safety on each of the computers in your home, not just one or two PCs. The good news is that Windows Live Family Safety is free.

Internet Content Filters at your ISP

Your Internet Service Provider (ISP) is the company that you pay each month to have Internet service. Some people get their Internet through their cable or telephone company. Many Internet Service Providers now offer a family or a business filtering system as an additional part of providing online access. One advantage to having filtering take place at your ISP is that it makes it much more difficult for members of your family to turn off the filtering system at your home computer. It also allows the filtering to move with you from computer to computer and from home to workplace. Check with your local ISP and see if they offer such a filtering system. Be prepared to pay anywhere from $5 to $15 a month for some ISP filtering services. As with software filters on your home computer, these services are not foolproof nor are they reliable replacements for parental involvement and intervention.

Domain Names Services (DNS)

As I mentioned above, when you go onto the Internet and you ask your web browser (Microsoft Internet Explorer, Mozilla Firefox, Google Chrome, etc.) to take you to a web site (www.nick.com) the web address (or Domain Name) is converted into an Internet Protocol address (IP address). In the case of www.nick.com the domain name is converted into its IP by another series of Internet servers called Domain Name Services servers (DNS). Usually the domain name translation occurs at your Internet Service Provider (ISP). Another way to provide filtering for your entire home or business network is to have your own DNS server watch and filter all of your family's network traffic and block items before they go any farther. Your ISP may provide internet content filtering and DNS services for you but if not, the OpenDNS project (www.opendns.com) can provide such DNS filtering. OpenDNS provides a free version which can allow you to direct all of your home's internet traffic to their DNS servers where they will monitor and filter all Internet requests. The good thing about setting up a filter like OpenDNS is that every device that uses your home internet, computers, laptops, cell phones, tablets, and even gaming systems will all be monitored and filtered with your OpenDNS settings. Because the filtering occurs after the request leaves your network you don't have to setup every user or device that is attached to your home network (like Microsoft's Family Safety). You will however have to figure out how to setup your home's Internet router/wireless router to point all traffic to OpenDNS. OpenDNS has tutorials on how to create a user account and help on how to setup your home router to use OpenDNS servers.

http://www.opendns.com/support/

Once your home network is pointed to the OpenDNS servers you can set up your own level of filtering, reporting and statistics. OpenDNS also has yearly subscription rates that will provide you with more function and value. Like the other filtering systems mentioned, DNS server filtering is not a complete solution to protecting your family while online. Consider it another tool in your toolbox of ways that you can help protect your kids while online.

From the CyberCop Case Files:
Who put a filter on my Internet?

A popular Internet Service Provider (ISP) that I often work with sells its customers one of the nationally renowned Internet filtering systems. The intended customers are both businesses and families and the monthly fee is nominal. One of the advantages to having filtering controlled at the ISP level is that no matter where the customer is located, when they use their ISP's service to connect with the Internet the filtering is handled at the ISP, not at the customer's computer. This makes it especially difficult for a person to bypass the filtering using methods such as password guessing, removing the filtering software, or by using another computer. Of course this will not work if they use someone else's Internet account.

The ISP filtering system had been paid for and was operating for a few months for a family. One day the support line received an upset call from the mother. She had recently purchased the filtering option and had it added to her monthly Internet billing statement. When she used her Internet account she realized that the filter was either not working or not present. Within a few minutes the ISP technical support staff was able to determine that the filtering system that once had been connected to her account had been recently ordered to be removed. The ISP's records indicated a call and email received several days earlier wherein her husband appeared to demand that the filtering system be removed and that his account be credited the difference.

The lady who called was amazed. Her husband had been out of town and could not have called nor emailed the ISP. He hardly ever used the Internet account. In fact, the only person who regularly used their Internet Account was their 14-year-old son. Could her son have called and impersonated his father? The ISP support staff pulled the suspect email from their data files and within a matter of minutes had determined that not only had the son most likely called the ISP pretending to be the father, the email that they received had been sent using the family's Internet account. Further, the email appeared to have been sent from the computer line in their son's bedroom (notice the computer was in the child's bedroom?). The email had been sent at approximately 3:35 p.m. on a weekday. The only person in the house at that time was the 14-year-old, who had come home from school to find that the Internet filter was active and he was being filtered.

The juvenile was appropriately punished and the Internet Service Provider changed its Internet Filtering Policies. Now if you want to change or turn off your Internet filtering, you must appear at the ISP headquarters in person and you must show proper identification before the account will be changed.

Internet Tracking Software

Suppose you just want to check up on where your family is going on the Internet. You have tried to check out their web browser cache folders and history data, but to no avail. You are sure that someone is trying to hide his or her Internet tracks from you. The easy answer is to use some Internet tracking software, also sometimes referred to as "keystroke logging" software. You can use the Windows Live Family Safety system in Windows 7 for free. You can also purchase computer software such as CyberSitter and Net Nanny that will log all computer activity so that you can later see what people are doing while at your computer. Other more robust and sneaky software is available to make it completely invisible to anyone else on the computer that you are monitoring their every move while online.

Do these programs work? You better believe they do. They work very well at spying on people using your family's computer. With many of these programs you can get everything that the person has done at the computer. I have used several software programs during my tenure as a law enforcement officer and one company stands out when it comes to recording a person's computer use. I recommend Spectorsoft's eBLASTER and Spector Pro software. (www.spectorsoft.com). Spectorsoft's suite of recording and monitoring software is wide and deep depending on your needs and wants. They make software for recording everything that goes on your computer, including every key typed, every program accessed, every web site visited, online chats, emails sent, and some of their software will even take screen snapshots of exactly what the person using your computer is doing without any clue that the computer is watching their every move. Their products can also send all of that information to you on a regular basis so you don't even need to be near the computer to see what is happening. They also make versions of the Macintosh Operating System.

I have had firsthand experience in several cases where people have installed such software on their computers to see cheating spouses, illegal activities by employees and in one case catch a suspect who was using someone else's computer to download child pornography.

I do not necessarily recommend that parents use this type of software on their children except after they have tried every other method at their disposal to protect their children and you have good reason to suspect that a child is likely to be putting himself or herself in danger. To install one of these programs on your family's computer means that you are going to violate a member of your family's trust and personal privacy. That is a pretty strong risk to be taking with someone that you love and care about. That is why there needs to be an extremely strong indication that your loved one is in danger from such things as an unknown Internet predator, the fear of possible suicide, or other dangerous activity. This shouldn't be used to see if your 13-year-old daughter is talking online with boys (believe me she already is and you don't need to wiretap her to figure that out). I had one case where the parents were genuinely concerned that their teenager was going to hurt herself. They were able to use the tracking software to determine she was in need of counseling and that she was extremely depressed and suicidal. They were able to get her into therapy and I am happy to report that she and her family are now doing very well.

If you just want to know if your kids are going to adult porn sites and you think that you may want to use this kind of software, I suggest you find another way to check up on your child. Try such things as looking in the cache folders and locating cookie files (see the chapter entitled "Checking your child's Web").

A cheap and easy way to see how the Internet is being used on your family's account is to take the time to check with your local

Internet Service Provider (ISP) and ask them for a copy of your Internet Account logs. Internet Account logs are data that your ISP normally keeps for the purposes of billing and account maintenance. It usually contains account activity which includes the time and date of connection and the Internet Protocol Address (IP) issued to the subscriber. This information does NOT include where the person went on the Internet or what they did while connected. Your ISP does not keep that information as a normal course of its business and frankly it is really none of their business anyway. Some ISPs allow you to check your Internet usage online. Check with your local provider for further details.

The information could be very useful for a parent who wants to make sure that their son or daughter isn't online when they should not be or to make sure that they are not online too long. The account log information from your ISP could also help you in determining if someone else has been using your account without your permission. Some Internet Service Providers may require that you pick up the account information in person and may even require that you provide proper identification. As the owner of the account, you have a right to see when and where your account is being used. If your ISP can not provide this information or says that they will not give you this information upon request, I suggest shopping around for another Internet Service Provider.

Email

Email is a wonderful tool. I use it a lot and I believe that it belongs right up there with regular mail (snail mail) and the telephone as one of best examples of technology that connects people together. Unfortunately, the mail service also brought us such things as death threats, the letter bomb and anthrax scares. The telephone gave us the crank call and the ever-popular nagging phone solicitors. Email also brings with it problems that parents need to be aware of.

At least once a week, I get a call from a parent who is extremely upset about an email referencing pornography that they or their child received. Usually after calming the caller down and extracting the necessary information from them I find that the email itself does not contain pornographic images, only typewritten references to pornography or links to adult web sites. The parent will also call when an email states that the sender refers to "teen" sex pictures and is afraid that the images are of children. Once again, after getting more information, the email is usually a bulk adult pornography email (also referred to as spam) and it is most likely referring to the 18 or 19 "barely legal" types of adult pornography. Words such as "teen" and "young" are marketing phrases used to entice some consumers to adult web sites. Like it or not, adult pornography (18 years of age and older) is legal in most areas of the country. In most of these cases it turns out that the family is a victim of large and efficient bulk emailing companies (spammers) who do not know them from the next guy (see the chapter entitled "Unsolicited emails (Spam)". That is not to say that we don't have cases of someone sending a child unsolicited porn over the Internet; however, in those cases, the victim usually knows who the suspect is or has been chatting with them online.

Email is another way that Internet predators, con artists and manipulators try to gain access to you and your children. It is usually not their preferred method of communication as it doesn't give them the immediate feedback and control that they like to have but it does keep them in touch with their victims. I had one case where the suspect met the victim in a chat room. He then developed a dialogue with her in one-on-one chat conversations. Next, he moved to exchanging emails with her and then he convinced the victim to only call him via telephone. He did that as he was concerned that her mother would find out about him if she ever checked her daughter's computer.

Do your kids have an email account?

The first item of information that you need to know is whether or not your child has an email address and do you know the password to his or her account? Most parents don't even realize that their kids have their own email accounts. You may not even have a computer in your home and your child may still have an email account that they have obtained from a friend's computer or at school. One of our local school districts actually encourages the students to use the free web-based email system from school. One of the school's system administrators told me that it is apparently too much of a hassle to deal with all of the students and their email accounts. I disagreed. If a school district can take the time to sign out books, assign lockers, and locker combinations, they certainly can take the time to provide each student with their own email along with a traceable username and password.

I was recently giving a presentation to a group of 200 middle school students. During the lecture, I asked them to raise their hands if they had their own email account. All of them raised their hands. When I asked them to put their hands down if their parents knew about their email account, most of them left their hands up. Many, however, indicated that their mom and dad did not know about their personal email let alone the account's password.

My advice here is pretty clear. Find out if your child has an email account or email accounts. I once located a juvenile who was sending death threats to another student and when he was questioned about his email account, he had five different email accounts. His parents did not know about any of them.

How do you find out? Try asking them. Most of the time, your child will tell you. Be honest with them as well. Let them know that you need to understand what the email account name is and what password it is that they use. Explain to your child (or teenager especially) that this is not about snooping into their personal lives, rather it's about having the keys necessary to protect them in the case of an emergency. It is your job to see that no harm comes to your child. Promise them that you will not enter or read their email unless they are missing, or are in danger.

Some of the more popular free email accounts include:

Google mail (gmail.com)
Yahoo mail (mail.yahoo.com)
Hotmail.com (hotmail.com)
AOL/AIM email (aim.com)

If you still suspect that your child might have an email account, check the computer(s) at home. A really "quick and dirty" way to see if your child has been using Hotmail or Gmail email is to open up your web browser's history file and see which web sites they have gone to (see the previous chapter entitled Web Caches and Web Histories for specific ways to check the web history). If you check in your web browser and you don't find anyone going to web sites such as Gmail, don't assume that someone isn't using Gmail or some other email service. Smarter kids (and Internet criminals) know about the history files and will attempt to hide their Internet activities by deleting the history files stored on the computer. I even had one suspect who instructed his 16-year-old victim how to delete certain files on her computer so as not to raise suspicions with her parents about their relationship.

Check with their school and any of their computer teachers about other email access. Explain to them that you need to be informed of any Internet or email accounts that your child has access to and what the user name and password is. If the school keeps those records or the records are kept off of the school grounds, find out who to contact. Get a name and a phone number. Call the person and confirm that this is the person who can get the information about your child's school computer and email activities (see the chapter entitled "Protecting your Internet child at school").

Let us say that you have discovered that your child has a web account, or maybe you have elected to set your child up with his or her own email account. One of my suggestions is to make sure that you and your child select an acceptable email address. You do not want their email name to say too much about him or her. Setting up an email account of briansmith12@hotmail.com tells people too much information. This one has Brian's full name and his possible age (12). Since we are only going to allow our kids to email people that we know and trust why advertise information that we don't need to? Don't have an email address that gives away personal and specific information about your child.

Be prepared, however, for some resistance regarding email names (especially from teenagers). I have a great deal of trouble trying to get kids to understand that email addresses, and other Internet nicknames, need to be non-specific, unidentifiable and non-sexual in nature. In a nutshell, the names need to be BORING, or at least creatively ambiguous. Why? It is because predators on the Internet know that psychologically people will tend to share something about themselves in the email names and nicknames that they choose while online. Internet perverts can use that information to identify potential targets as well as use the information to their advantage. They will use the fact that your child has the email nickname of "Hockeyplr14" to open up a dialog about playing hockey. They may also clue in on your child's age (the 14 in Hockeyplr14) if you are freely advertising it.

I had another case where the parent was shocked to learn that their child had her own email address and that her 15-year-old daughter was using the address of "babyblu15" for meeting people online. Her daughter at first failed to understand that by using that name she was making herself more vulnerable and attractive to the older men who were corresponding with her. In this case, the person she was writing to turned out to be an online predator and child pornographer.

Personal child safety experts ask that parents don't put their child's name on any outer clothing or backpacks as it allows suspects to key in on your child's name. The same goes for the Internet. Don't give people access to the kind of information that might identify your child online (or in real life for that matter).

Check your younger children's email with them. If your teenager checks his or her own email account then set up some basic rules.

One of the best email systems that I have found for children is one called Zoobuh. Zoobuh.com provides a safe email system for your kids and it puts the power of checking and knowing what your kids are emailing and sending in your hands (Figure 42).

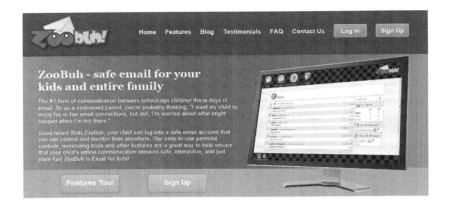

Figure 42

Zoobuh.com allows you to create email accounts for your children while giving full control over the content and the way that their email works. With Zoobuh you can control everything about the email account from when they can check their email, to who can send or receive email from them. They have built in filters that you can set so your children cannot send or receive such items as images, videos, mp3 music files, etc. You can even act as your own monitor and receive every email that your child gets or sends to your own email account. You can then decide if the email should be allowed out of Zoobuh. My son has been using a zoobuh.com email account for several years and it works very well. Zoobuh.com is very reasonably priced and costs only $1 per month, per email account.

Email Rules for Families

1) Don't open any email if you do not know who the person is who sent it.

2) Teach your children to report to you any email that they receive that is threatening, offensive, derogatory, or makes

116

them uncomfortable. In the case of the Internet Predator, the emails will usually not begin in an overtly sexual manor; however they can quickly become serious if the pervert begins looking for some "shock" value.

3) Never respond to any offensive or unsolicited email (see Unsolicited Email/Spam). Report offensive emails to your Internet Service Provider. There are two reasons for this. The first reason is that by replying to a message you have just informed the person who sent the original message that you are a real person with a valid email account. Your email address can then be used again, given to others, or even sold to bulk emailers (spam). The other reason for not replying is that if you reply you are telling that person that you can be manipulated. It says that you can be taunted into responding to an email. It puts the bad guy in the driver's seat. He has gotten you to do something that you would not normally do. It may "feel good" at first to send an email telling the idiot what you think of him and his email, however, the suspect does not see it that way. He sees it as another opportunity to engage you with more correspondence. It sounds strange but it is true.

I get calls every week from people who have received upsetting emails in one form or another. In some of the cases the victim got upset at the content and responded to the email. In nearly every case, the suspect continued to try and contact the victim. When the victim does not reply, it gives the suspect only two possibilities. Either the email did not reach them, or they aren't doing what he wanted. In either situation, you win and they don't. Don't let them win.

4) Don't allow your child to meet anyone that they have corresponded with through email (The same goes for the web, chat, newsgroups, social networking site, or any other Internet connection).

5) Don't send any email that you wouldn't want the entire world to see. You and your child should know that once an email leaves your computer, you have no way to stop it. Like a bullet shot from a gun, once you send an email you cannot take it back (see the chapter entitled "What is... Email?").

From the CyberCop Case Files:
The Case of the Email Mistake

I was once approached by a fellow police officer who told me that her son had received a death threat via email. She later brought me the email which read:

```
    [name   deleted],   I   am   very
unpleased,  therefore  I  think  I  will
kill  u  when  u  least  expect  it,  when
u'r  mom's  not  around  because  she's  a
cop

 -U'll  Never  guess
```

Given that the email was specific in its message, and the fact that the person obviously knew his mom was a police officer, I believed that we needed to follow this case up and do so as quickly as possible. I also suspected that given the poor grammar and the Internet chat lingo that was used ("u" instead of "you") the author of this letter was likely juvenile. In order to determine the exact location of the email I would need to see the original email and the email's header information.

The next day my fellow officer brought her son into the police station and I sat him down in front of one of my Internet computers and asked him to pull the email back up from his Hotmail email account. Once he logged into his account I clicked on the Hotmail menu bar which read "options." Under the options screen I selected "preferences." I then located the selection for "message headers." This I set to "Full" which allowed me to view the full message headers for his email. Once the full header preferences were set, he located the threatening email and we printed out the message again but this time with the full email headers.

With the full email header information we were able to determine that the email originated from an Internet account located in his town. This was some additional news that was unnerving as it meant that the suspect was nearby and had physical access to the family.

After visiting my local Judge and obtaining a search warrant for the Internet Service Provider, the ISP was able to use the email header information to determine which of its customers had sent the email. The news was unexpected. The suspect was one of the victim's best friends. Further investigation (i.e. I called the friend's mom), revealed that the friend had been "goofing around" and sent the email to his buddy as a joke. After sending the email, the friend realized that it wasn't being taken as a joke and was afraid of getting into trouble. In turn, he avoided saying anything about sending the email. The officer did not press charges and the matter was handled appropriately by the families with the suspect spending the rest of the summer doing free lawn care for the entire neighborhood.

Unsolicited Emails (Spam)

If you have an email account then you most likely have experienced emails from people that you don't know and in most cases don't want. These unwanted Internet emails are unsolicited junk (bulk) sales pitches and are often referred to as "Spam." Internet legend has it that the term Spam is sometimes a reference to a Monty Python comedy skit set in a diner that served the processed meat known as Spam to Viking customers constantly chanting "SPAM, SPAM, SPAM!." I don't know why the luncheon meat (www.spam.com) gets such a bad rap. It doesn't appear to have anything to do with unsolicited emails; however, the name appears to have stuck.

Unsolicited emails may seem to just be annoying but relatively safe. In reality they are not completely harmless. These unsolicited emails often contain solicitations for illegal activities, scams (get rich quick schemes), pornography, computer viruses and material inappropriate for children (as well as some adults). They clog up your Internet Service Provider's email servers and they fill up your email inbox.

How to avoid getting unsolicited email

The best way to avoid receiving unsolicited emails in the first place is to not give out your email address. That is easy to say but difficult to do for most of us. Here are some suggestions to try and limit the number of unsolicited emails (spam) that you get, but don't expect it to completely stop anytime soon.

1) Don't put your child's email address on any web pages. This includes your personal web pages, your child's web pages, your social networking sites (Facebook, MySpace,

etc.) or any other web page that can be accessed from the Internet. What the bulk emailers (spammers) have are little computer programs called "bots" that search the Internet and the World Wide Web looking for valid email addresses written into the web page's code. The bulk emails can then use your child's email address to send email or even sell your email address to others. If your child's email address is published online then it is only a matter of time before their email address will begin receiving unsolicited email.

2) Don't allow your child to sign up for free stuff online, or post to other web sites or to Newsgroups (See the chapter entitled "What is a newsgroup"). The bulk emails regularly grab people's emails from the newsgroups and use them to send their advertising.

3) Don't allow your child to give out his or her email to anyone else without first checking with you. This includes web sites that require your child to give them any information about your child.

4) Make sure that you are running a commercial anti-virus software package (AVG, Norton Anti-Virus, Avast, etc) and make sure that the virus definitions are up to date. Many illegal spammers actually do so from other unsuspecting people's personal and network server computers. They take over computers using virus or Trojan horse programs that turn your computer into a conduit to send out spam emails.

How to curtail unsolicited email

Once you begin getting unsolicited email, it is very difficult to stop the flow of email traffic into your mailbox. There are several things that you can try to do to curb some of the unwanted emails.

1) Do not respond to an unsolicited email. In doing so you are telling the sender that a real person gets mail at this account and they in turn can use that information to sell your email address to others. Even if the unsolicited email has something to the effect of "to be removed from this email list, please send an email to the following email address..." do not respond. In many cases the email address is either bogus or is another way for the bulk emailers to get more information on you or your child's email address.

2) Check with your Internet Service Provider (ISP). Some ISPs are very sensitive to unsolicited emails and their customer's requests to curtail it. From the ISP's perspective, these unwanted emails can be a strain on their own systems simply by the sheer magnitude of the numbers of unsolicited emails that are being handled by their computers. If the ISP can limit these unwanted emails then their own systems work more efficiently and they can spend more time helping their paying customers rather than dealing with non-paying email spammers. Some ISPs will block emails from a particular Internet ISP or computer if they receive enough complaints from customers. Be prepared to give your ISP the entire spam email.

3) Set up your email program to filter messages. Most email programs will allow you to create filters to check your incoming emails for possible unsolicited email and will attempt to filter them out. Email filters can help but be aware that they can be tricky and time consuming to setup.

Chat rooms

Cases involving chat rooms and the exploitation of our children dates back to the very beginnings of the world wide web. One of the first cases I even learned about was nearly 20 years ago and it happened while I was still in the police academy. The case involved a 15-year-old female who met a 40-year-old adult male in an Internet chat room and. The two of them began a series of conversations that eventually lead to them meeting in a parking lot of our local library. The victim had told mother that she had to "study". The two of them met socially several times and soon began having sexual relations with each other. The girl eventually admitted the incident to friend who later informed the authorities. When the man was identified, it was discovered that he was a 40-year-old computer network administrator. His computers at home and at work were examined and were found to contain segments of their chat conversations. This case was our first, but it wasn't our last.

A couple of years ago, I was asked by a local prosecutor to demonstrate how chat rooms operate. He wanted to see what all of the buzz was about. I told him I would be happy to oblige him and to come over to my office.

We logged into an AOL Instant Messenger chat area to see what we could find. My plan was to go to any number of the teen or kids-oriented rooms and wait to see what happened. I wasn't in a particular room for more than five minutes when a stranger asked if I wished to engage in a one to one chat with him. I agreed and within three minutes, the predator was asking to engage in online sex chat. He also offered to send us photographs of nude children engaged in sexual acts. Needless to say the suspect was a bit surprised when we informed him that we were with law enforcement and wanted to have a real face-to-face discussion with him regarding his current sexual desires. He didn't believe us at first. We had to send him some actual legal passages referencing the sexual abuse of minors' statutes and the transportation of child pornography before he got a clue and immediately logged off. I suspect he was at home deleting his child pornography collection and hoping that the police didn't knock on his door. I'm also quite certain that within a week or so he was back "cruising" the chat rooms looking for his next victim.

I wish that I could say that these examples are rare but they really aren't. In computer crime investigation classes being presented all over the country, instructors are going into chat rooms and are being "picked up" by predators on a regular basis. I once did a lecture to a group of sexual assault investigators where I got so many perverts online asking to pick me up that I could not keep them all straight! All of this was long before NBC Dateline's "To Catch a Predator" television series came into being.

Some chat systems have attempted to help curb the problem by having moderators within their chat system and by having real people moderating their teen and kid chat rooms. This appears to help when the child stays in a room and does not go elsewhere or as long as the child forbids strangers from messaging him or her (Instant Messenger). Unfortunately not many children are able to stay within those bounds and without parental intervention an online predator will eventually approach them.

Other chat systems are just as problematic (if not worse). Yahoo chat rooms and the Internet Relay Chat (IRC) for example may have some chat rooms that may be worthwhile and could be a source for information; however, the vast majority of them are quite different. For example, rooms in the IRC chat system give you little or no information useful in determining the quality of the room or the members contained within. Could rooms like #chat-world (with 134 chatters inside), or #cancer-survivors (4 people) be safe places? Maybe. How about the rooms such as #!!!!!100%teensexpics, or #100%animalsexpics, or how about

#rapesex? Are these safe places for you or your children? I don't think so.

Having spent time in hundreds of chat rooms while investigating Internet crimes, I have to say that chat rooms are one Internet activity where parents need to "put their foot down" and not allow children at any age to become involved. This may seem like a harsh proposition. However, chatting and chat rooms are the one area of the Internet where an unknown person has the ability to engage in direct, one-on-one communication with your child. Concerned parents would never allow their child to have an unlimited number of long-distance telephone calls with someone they don't know. There is no difference with chat rooms. As a matter of fact chat rooms are far worse. At least with a telephone call your child might be able to tell if the person on the other side is a boy or a girl, a man or a woman and possibly how old the person was. With online chatting, your child cannot hear the other person, which is a vital tool in a child's ability to sense when someone poses a threat to them. The person on the other side holds all of the cards and your child is at a serious disadvantage. The online perpetrator knows what to say to your child. They don't always come straight out and tell your child what it is they want from them. They take their time and quickly learn how to give the victim what they need in order to manipulate the situation to their advantage. In the criminal arena, we call it "grooming" the victim.

Unfortunately, these days nearly every computer and cell phone has chat programs on them. With the advent of social networking sites such as Facebook, chat is freely available to your kids 7 days a week, 24 hours a day.

That is why I seriously suggest that you not allow your child to chat online except when the chat is under an extremely controlled environment. Such a scenario would be in the case where you are with your kids during chats, or possible in a situation at school where the students are in a controlled conference/chat with another classroom. Check with your child's school and see if they offer such programs. If not, consider lending a hand to help volunteer and monitor.

"Unsupervised Internet chatting for children is a high risk, low value situation and I don't recommend it."

Now before I get inundated with people telling me how their lives were made better through chat rooms and how they met their significant other through the online chat system, let me say this. If you, as an adult, want to chat and meet the people that you chat with, that is your prerogative. If chatting is your thing, more power to you (and good luck). If you choose to chat, please try to be smart and stay safe. I personally find online chatting to be boring, dangerous for children, and lacking any amount of reliable and honest feedback. Please be aware that what you do as an adult and what you should allow your child to do while online are two completely different things. Kids and unsupervised chatting simply do not mix.

Guarding your Child's Personal Information

With the advent of the Internet, the amount of information that is available online is simply incredible. There are more and more databases with information regarding individual citizens than ever before. Personal information is being bought and sold often without the knowledge of the individuals listed. As companies continue to enter the Internet age, more and more information about us is being provided to the general public by well-meaning and by uninformed organizations. I'm not going to debate here the pros or cons of whether or not it is proper for companies to buy, sell, or distribute information regarding other people and their activities (although I am opposed to it). What I want is for you as a parent is to realize that the chances of there being information about you and your family available out on the Internet is extremely high. Your job as concerned parents is to try and minimize and control that information as best you can.

A case in point was a simple non-scientific test that I did a couple of years ago. I wanted to make a point to some of my fellow police officers that they needed to be wary of what kind of information there was out on the Internet about them. I wanted to show them what kinds of personal information a bad guy could learn about a police officer and their family. Most police officers I know take steps to carefully protect their personal information. I wanted to see if even the most careful and safety conscious cops could be located and what kinds of information I could easily and legally gather using only the Internet as my resource.

I randomly selected five police officers' names for my study. Some of the names were of senior police officers, and some were new to the police force. I began by using some of the major Internet Search engines (Google.com, Bing.com, Yahoo.com, etc).

Simply entering the person's name and a state often gave me several good areas to go to on the web to learn more about my subjects. I quickly found that one officer had an entire web page with photos of his whole family on it! This was something that I recommended he discontinue doing, and he quickly removed the images.

Next I wanted to see if I could locate the homes and personal telephone numbers of my test subjects. I went and checked out some of the phone listing and address search systems such as www.spokeo.com, www.zabasearch.com, and people.yahoo.com.

Even I was surprised with the results of my search. Within 20 minutes of beginning my experiment I had the personal home telephone numbers of all five of my police officers and I obtained the correct home addresses of 4 of the 5 subjects. I published the results of my experiment in our Police Newsletter (minus the officer's personal information of course). I was attempting to impress upon my co-workers that they needed to be aware that this sort of loss of privacy is here to stay and to be extra cautious when answering the door of their house to strangers. There is no telling who might be at the front door these days. This is the same advice that I now give you. Conduct your own personal experiment. Try going online and learning what you can about yourself and your family. You might just be surprised about what is really available online and who might have access to it.

In an attempt to protect the rights and privacy of our youngest citizens, the United States Congress recently enacted the "Children's Online Privacy Protection Act of 1998." This act was created to try to protect the personal rights of children who use the Internet by mandating what online web site operators could and could not do with information regarding juveniles (www.coppa.org).

Web sites that cater to, or are directed at children had to post on their sites what kinds of information they collect from children under the age of 13 (name, address, email address, etc.). The web site must also say specifically what they will do with that information, and whether or not they will give or sell that child's information to others. The law tries to require the web sites to obtain parental consent to collect this information and exactly how it can be used. Failure to comply with the Children's Online Privacy Protection Act can bring sanctions against the web site owners and operators, including legal action and fines.

I see the Children's Online Privacy Protection Act of 1998 (which actually took effect on April 21, 2000) as a step in the right direction. It was a small step, but a step nonetheless. This law is only directed at web sites (not the entire Internet- newsgroups, chat, email), and exclusively covers children under the age of 13. That means that teenagers are not protected by this legislation.

There are many Internet filtering software packages that can be purchased which attempt to limit what kind of information your child can type and send to a web site or out via email. That too is a good thing, but it is not always 100% effective.

What can parents do about protecting their child's personal privacy and information while on the Internet? Here are some of my suggestions.

1. Find out if your child has a web page or a social networking site.

2. Figure out what kind of information they may have put there.

3. Review their web pages and edit them for personal information that you do not want published (full name, physical address, descriptions of your child, photographs, etc.) If you do not know whether or not your child has a

web site, ask them. Ask their friends.

4. Ask their teacher if your son or daughter has a school sanctioned web page and what personal information has been posted there.

5. Still don't know? Many free Internet web page companies and Social Networking sites create an environment that allows your kids to create a web page without a parent's knowledge or consent. Such free pages include but most certainly are not limited to:

www.facebook.com
www.myspace.com
www.bebo.com
www.myyearbook.com

While recently on one these web sites, I searched for "Alaska" and "13 year old." I quickly located several kids in our area including a 13 year old female juvenile who was kind enough to advertise her name, date of birth, her location, her descriptors (height, weight, hair color, etc.) and the kinds of things that she likes to do. She has unwittingly given any potential predators out there, all of the information they need to begin attempting to correspond and to develop a relationship with her. I'm fairly sure that her parents are unaware of her web pages and the large amount of information that she was unknowingly making available to anyone with access to the Internet.

When I joined another site under the guise of being a "teenager," I located dozens of different pages that had been created by some of our local teenagers. Many of their web pages came complete with their real names, addresses, email accounts, schools, and even photographs! It was like one stop shopping for an Internet predator.

Make it a family rule not to give out personal information when joining a web site, email, or posting anything to the Internet. Mom or dad must first approve all information that is going to be sent out. This also includes when signing up for "free" giveaways, free email accounts and all online promotions.

Cyber Bullying

Next to unsolicited porn emails the most common telephone call that I receive from upset parents is the "cyber bullying" or harassment of their son or daughter from someone via the Internet. The parent usually calls to report that their child is getting nasty emails from this known or unknown person and the situation is described as "out-of-control." The conversation then turns to the "so what are the cops going to do about this?" It is at this point that I begin a series of questions aimed at determining the form and the extent of the harassment. By determining the form and type of harassment that the victim is exposed to we can then develop a plan of action which may or may not include police intervention.

What form does the harassment take?

Is the suspect communicating through email? Most of the reported harassment that I see is in the form of emails, usually originating from free email systems such as Hotmail, Gmail, or Yahoo mail.

If the suspect is using some other means, such as web pages, or classified ads (like Craigslist.com) to indirectly harass the victim, I may now have more information to go on. I have had cases where the suspect has taken the time to create a web page (usually on a free web site) where they have placed the victim's personal information, email, home number and the like for all to see on the Internet. I had one case where a jilted ex-boyfriend put a web site up referencing his old girlfriend's home telephone number and told the visitors there that she was really into "battery operated devices." Another method used by these cyber-ex's (or relation terrorists as I like to call them) are to place classified ads online and leave the victim's name, telephone number or email for quick responses to her "ad." I had one gentleman do this after only a single date with a girl. After refusing to see him again, she began getting emails and photographs from sexual deviants all over the globe. I actually sent the suspect an email and got my first confession from him via email (which I later followed up with a telephone call and eventually formal criminal charges). He said that he did it because she refused to see him again. He also promised to never do it again. I formally charged him with harassment despite his promise to leave her alone.

What is the extent of the harassment?

This can be the trickiest part of the case. If the harassment is in the form of email, then the frequency and the wording of the emails can be very important, at least from the view of building a criminal case. Is it just one email or are the emails more frequent? I have had cases where there has been one and only one email received. Those types of cases are very difficult to work, especially if the writer was "vague" or did not specifically threaten to hurt the victim. Multiple emails do tend to raise the level of concern. I had one case where the victim had been receiving emails for over 6 months and the frequency of the emails had been increasing as time went on. The longer a pattern continues and the more specific the harassment becomes, the greater the level of the threat. That is one reason why I mentioned earlier that one should never respond to unsolicited emails (see the chapter entitled Unsolicited Emails (SPAM)). Responding to such attempts to control and upset you is exactly what the author is trying to do. Most annoying emails stop after there is no "reaction" or response from the victim. It is the continuing and progressive pattern of activity that is the most worrisome. That is not to say that a single threat should not be taken seriously. It only takes one threat to place a person in fear for their life.

What is the intent of the harassment?

Is the harassing communication meant to annoy? Is it trying to scare the victim? Is the communication specifically threatening? Was the author trying to remain anonymous? There are no easy answers when it comes to trying to determine just what is going on inside of the mind of someone who does this. One of the best rules that I can give parents is this:

"The more frequent or specific the threat,
the greater the risk of harm to you or your child."

If the communication is frequent then this alone should raise some red flags for parents. If the situation specifies a particular threat "I'm going to shoot you" or "I'll cut your throat" then that is a direct threat and is a crime in most jurisdictions. "You'll get yours" may be a threat to some people; however it is not always a specific "threat" or assault per se. This does not mean that you should not ever take a non-specific threat seriously (you should). One does, however, have to be more cautious when the suspect has taken the time to fantasize or plan out exactly what he or she wants to see happen and he or she spells it out in a specific manner.

If the suspect is trying to be completely anonymous and the victim has no idea who the suspect is, then generally the risk of harm is less than if the suspect makes his or her identity known to the victim. If the author takes no actions to hide his or her identity then the situation is potentially more dangerous. The level of technological sophistication and means of the suspect can also affect this determination.

If you know who the suspect is then one of the first things that I recommend is for the victim to consider obtaining a restraining order. Nearly all states have a system for acquiring and serving a restraining order. Many of them can be very specific as to the nature of the order. The order can contain a passage which includes that the suspect is to have no contact with the victim, including via the Internet. Restraining orders are not bulletproof vests, nor are they 100% effective. They are just a piece of paper that is essentially a judge telling this idiot to knock off the childish behavior or face civil and criminal repercussions. Restraining orders are often a real world wake-up call for the knucklehead out there who thinks he or she is righteous in continuing to harass inside and outside of the cyber world. In many cases, the harassing activity stops after the first restraining order. If the harassment doesn't stop then a restraining order probably wouldn't have done much good anyway. It can be excellent evidence for a police officer to use in opening up a potential case of stalking.

If the suspect is unknown to the victim, then tracing the email is one possible solution. If you can locate the source of the email, then sending (or better yet calling) the suspect's ISP or email provider is one way to make things difficult for them. Most ISPs and email systems have very specific rules against harassing or threatening emails from their systems and most of them will shut a suspect's email account down if you can provide them with enough evidence of a violation within their system.

Let's look at an example of cyber harassment where the suspect is using an email address of dorky@notyahoomail.com. How do you know whom to contact at this email company (NotYahooMail.com)? One way is to use the Internet Whois system to try and determine the operator (or administrator) of a particular Internet company. You can even locate Whois information via the World Wide Web. You can use any number of web sites that can search and lookup the owner of web sites, IP addresses and the like. Several of these sites include:

whois.domaintools.com
www.whois.net

Another site to locate the owners of a particular Internet computer is a domain name company such as Network Solutions (www.networksolutions.com) or Go Daddy (www.godaddy.com). These sites are some of the companies that are responsible for selling and maintaining a large amount of the web site addresses on the Internet.

A check to see who runs the email system for our suspect (dorky@notyahoomail.com) would look something like this (Figure 43):

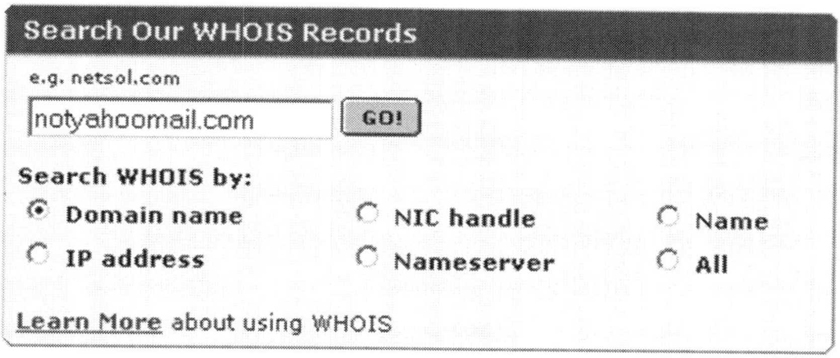

Figure 43

If the company is a valid organization we should receive some information about them and possibly a list of who to contact at their firm (Figure 44).

SEARCH RESULTS

```
Registrant:
NotYahooMail Corporation
    1345 Nockturnal Way
    Los Angeles, CA 90027  US
```

```
Domain Name: NotYahooMail.com

Administrative contact, technical
Contact, Billing Contact:
Records, Custodian of  (COR999)
abuse@notyahoomail.com
1345 Nockturnal Way
Los Angles, CA 90027  US
(605) 555-1234        (fax) 605 555-4321
```

Figure 44

I would attempt to contact the owners first by telephone and
also by email using the information given in the Whois results
(Figure 44). Be prepared to send or fax them copies of the
harassing correspondence, including any and all email header
information.

Another place to go and search out the suspect is with search
engines such as Google (groups.google.com). There is always a
possibility that the suspect may have posted to some various
websites or newsgroups using his name or email address (for more
information about newsgroups see the chapter entitled "What are...
Newsgroups"). Which areas of the Internet the suspect frequents
and what he or she posts can be very telling and may lead to
discovering the bad guy or bad gal's true identity.

Cyberbullying/Harassment and the Law

You need to be aware that some harassing or cyber bullying
activities in the Internet may not be a crime in your area (yet). In
my local area we have more computers per capita tied to the
Internet than nearly any other state. We have laws against
physically abusing children, child pornography, and other types of
crimes that can be facilitated online. What we didn't have up until
this last year was a state law against using the Internet to harass or

annoy another person. You need to check your current local, county, or state departments of law to see if your area has adequate legal recourse against Internet harassment.

Internet Stalking and the Law

I am pleased to report that officers in our state do appear to have adequate laws governing the non-consensual and repeated contact of victims by their perpetrators (Stalking). Please take the time to check your local and state laws about stalking and be sure to find out if the Internet is plainly spelled out in your local laws.

If you find that you or your family are not being adequately protected simply because of the lack of legislation involving cyber bullying or stalking please take the time to voice your concerns to you city, county and state representatives. Let them know your concerns and give them suggestions on how to make families safer when it comes to Internet harassment and other forms of cybercrime.

From the CyberCop case Files:
The Web Pages from Hell

A couple of years ago I was asked to assist one of our Domestic Violence Investigators on a case involving Internet harassment. A victim reported that she had been receiving sexually explicit emails and a series of telephone calls from a variety of men from around the world. These telephone calls would occur at all hours of the day and night. She was understandably frightened and upset and she suspected that her old boyfriend "Bob" might be behind the harassment. The victim had a restraining order out on Bob, which mandated that he have no direct or indirect contact with her. If we could prove that Bob was behind these emails and telephone calls we might be able to arrest him for violating the restraining order, in addition to a possible charge of harassment.

We had two ways to try to make this particular case. One method would be low tech and the other high tech. The Cybercop that I am, I voted for the high tech method which meant that I would run traces on the emails and contact email and ISP providers in an attempt to locate the person responsible at the source. This work would include a couple of days and probably a couple of search warrants, but I was sure that we would get our man. The Domestic Violence Investigator suggested that we first try a low tech method to solve this case. "If he is doing this kind of thing now, then he sure as hell has done this sort of thing in the past" said the senior investigator. He insisted that we try and locate Bob's ex-girlfriends and see what they could tell us about him.

Trying the low tech method first, we proceeded to search for and locate one of his old girlfriends. As it turned out, his previous girlfriend also had a current restraining order against Bob. When questioned about Bob's other ex-girlfriend and the strange emails she had been receiving, this woman explained to us that Bob had set up an adult web site with our victim's personal information posted on it. He included her full name, home address, telephone number, email address and all of her alleged sexual preferences. The web page continued by asking for nude photos and said stating that the victim enjoyed phone-sex. When this former girlfriend was questioned by the senior investigator, she answered, "He showed me. He showed me the web site. Told me he was pissed off at her and that he wanted to see her suffer."

With that information we easily obtained a search warrant for Bob's house. Bob was not pleased to see us. At first he denied that he had anything to do with the harassing email and telephone calls to the victim. He knew that there was a restraining order and said he wasn't going to risk getting into more trouble by violating the order (did I mention that almost EVERYONE lies to the police?). When we informed Bob that we had a search warrant for his house and for his computer he admitted he set up the web page with the victim's information. We later learned that his own company takes a dim view of their employees harassing people from their office. Bob used to work for a large oil company but he doesn't work there anymore. Charges against Bob for violation of the restraining orders and harassment were also forwarded to the prosecutor office.

Runaway/Missing Children

It is a parent's worst fear. Your child is gone. Have they runaway or have they been taken? Will they be all right? The only thing that the parents know is that their child is gone. When a child is missing it is a concern for everyone. This includes the family, the police, and the community. All of us need to be concerned and we all need to get involved.

With the advent of the Internet there is an added dimension to an already confusing situation. If you have been paying attention as you have been reading along you know that if your children are given unrestricted access to the Internet, a great number of influences can be brought to bear against them. The World Wide Web, email, newsgroups and chat rooms all can bring your child into contact with other people, both good and bad.

When a child comes up missing it is a parent's worst nightmare. Although this book is directed at keeping your kids Internet Safe, the actual disappearance of a child is the one thing that we are all trying to avoid. That is why I want parents, friends, and family to be aware of the possible Internet connection when it comes to cases of missing or runaway kids. I am not blaming the Internet for kids running away or being taken by predators. The Internet is merely a facilitator in some of these cases. I do however want you take the Internet connection into consideration should one day someone you love turn up missing.

When your child is first discovered to be missing, the U.S. Department of Justice (DOJ) Office of Juvenile Justice and I concur that parents need to take the following steps as soon as possible.

1) Search the house and immediate area for any place where your child might be hiding or playing.

2) Call the police and notify them of your child's disappearance.

3) Ask that the police issue a "locate" or an All-Points Bulletin (APB), or an Amber Alert for your child and have the authorities enter your child's information into the National Crime Information Center (NCIC).

4) Limit the access to your home, car, and the area where your child was last seen until law enforcement arrives.

5) Request and obtain the name, and telephone number of the officer or investigator assigned to your child's case. Obtain their internal case management number.

6) Provide investigators with complete facts and details related to your child's disappearance. Be prepared to describe to law enforcement complete details about your child and their disappearance.

7) Provide a complete detailed description of your child including a recent photograph, specific descriptors (height, weight, hair color, eye color, scars, marks, tattoos, mannerisms, clothing, etc.).

8) Provide investigators with a list of all of your child's friends, acquaintances, teachers, coaches, and neighbors. Include their addresses and telephone numbers. Let the officers know about any recent suspicious activities or recent changes in the family dynamics.

9) Tell the police about any medical or psychological problems. Is your child on any medications?

10) Be prepared to assist law enforcement with any requests or

directions that they request from you, even if they don't seem relevant at the time. The police often have multiple avenues of resources working on finding your child and you may not be aware that simple things that you do and say can help them better focus on what is needed to find your loved one.

For more information about coping with the disappearance of a child I recommend obtaining a free copy of the National Center for Missing and Exploited Children (NCMEC) publication entitled "Just in case... Guidelines in case your child might someday be missing," This free publication can be obtained online at their web site and is available in both English, Spanish, and Vietnamese versions at:

http://www.missingkids.com/en US/publications/NC17.pdf

If you suspect that the missing child (or even an adult for that matter) has been spending time online and they have a computer and/or an Internet account, I recommend that the following steps also be taken as soon as possible.

1) Secure the item(s) by not allowing anyone else to touch the computer, laptop, or cell phone. That means that no one is to use the computer in any way. They are not to open any files or go "poking" around to see what they can find. By doing so you can inadvertently destroy valuable information that could assist authorities in locating your child.

2) If the computer is on, don't turn it off.

3) If the computer is off, don't turn it on.

4) Let the police and the investigators know which devices your child uses and give them every detail that you can

about your child's Internet use. This would include a list of their Internet friends, their email account(s) and all of the passwords that your son or daughter uses. Give the authorities any nicknames or Internet "handles" that your child may use. If you know that your kid has a web page or social networking page, give that to the police as well.

5) If you suspect that the Internet may have something to do with your child's disappearance, make sure that this information is readily apparent to the police. Many police departments are not as computer savvy as they can be and the initial responding officers may not see the computer as a viable resource filled with evidence. Have the police examine these items as soon as possible.

6) Have someone contact your Internet Service Provider (ISP) and if appropriate your child's cellular provider to get a complete set of account usage and call logs. Additionally request that they provide and preserve all account information, including any emails that may still be present in the account. This information could prove to have vital information regarding your child. You have a right to obtain this information from your online accounts. You do, after all, pay them and they are your accounts.

I was once asked to look for clues on a computer involving a teenager who had been missing for a week. The juvenile was thought by many to have run away from home. The investigators were hoping that I might be able to locate some information as to where the girl might have gone. Talking with the parents revealed that she often used the family's computer and spent time checking her email and chatting online with several friends. Searching the family's computer I found nothing out of the ordinary; in fact, I was able to determine from the computer that the last time she had checked her email was the night before she disappeared.

After locating the family's email provider I asked them to run a check of their email log files for her account. Most Internet Service Providers (ISP) and Internet email services keep data records of Internet and email usage. These logs include such information as the date and times that the account was used, and the length of time that the person was connected to the Internet.

In this case I was hoping that the email provider could tell me the last time that her personal email account was used and what Internet Protocol (IP) number was assigned to the email. If the missing girl had simply run away and was hiding out at a friend's house she would most likely be checking her email from somewhere. I was hoping that her Internet use would lead us right to her. Unfortunately, when I received the account log information I learned that the girl had not sent, received, or even used her favorite email account in the past week. I told the case officer of my findings and told him that I believed that the missing girl was most likely in some serious danger. The girl was later discovered dead, a victim of a suicide.

From the CyberCop case files:
The Long Distance Runaway

One of the first Internet related cases that I worked when I was a new and young officer was that of a young girl who had run away from home. Even present day, a 12-year-old girl running away from home is not unusual. This case was a 12-year-old-girl who ran away from her home in southern California and was determined to make it all the way to Alaska.

I first received a telephone call from the missing girl's distraught father. They lived in a suburb on the outskirts of Los Angeles, California. According to her father, "Clara" had been spending time with her grandmother in San Diego during the summer. While her grandmother was at work during the day, Clara had the run of the house, including access to grandmother's Internet account. The scenario that the father later pieced together was that Clara would spend her days in Internet Chat rooms. There she met a man named "Royce" who was apparently from Alaska. They soon began corresponding via email and later developed "feelings" for each other.

Summer over, dad returned from work one day to discover that Clara was gone. She had left a note saying that she was "in love" and had left to be with her "boyfriend". Her parents searched her room and found printed out emails and letters from "Royce" in Alaska. They were able to have a police investigator search their home computer where they located email and address information, which led them to contact me.

I was able to use this information to locate the residence of the suspect, "Royce." Royce turned out to be an 18-year-old male who lived with his parents in the northern part of the city. I immediately dispatched one of the biggest, meanest officers I know to go to the residence and look for the missing 12-year-old. He was unable to locate the girl at the residence. The suspect and his parents insisted that they did not even know she was coming. The officer kindly explained to Royce and his parents the criminal ramifications of potentially harboring a runaway: child endangerment, unlawful exploitation of a minor and the Sexual Abuse of Minor. Royce and his parents were asked to call the police if she ever showed up.

Four hours later our dispatch center received a telephone call from Royce's residence. Clara had arrived and was outside their door. Apparently the officer had made such an impression upon the family that they were hesitant to even let her inside. Officers arrived and took Clara into protective custody. Her father was notified and he soon arrived on the next available flight from California. Clara was reunited with her father and entered into a lengthy discussion between the two of them as they flew back to California together.

Children as Prey: The Sexual Assault of Minors

It is difficult, if not impossible, to look at your children and see them as a potential victim. Most right-minded parents would have a hard time doing that. Sexual predators on the other hand look at your children in many different ways. They look at them in a sexual way (they often use the term "sensual"). They look at them as a way to fulfill their own wants and desires. They spend a great deal of time fantasizing about kids. They spend time trying to talk to kids. They want to interact with kids. They want to make themselves feel like they are helping kids, not hurting them. They want to see children in photographs and in movies. They want to set up actual meetings with kids. They want to teach kids about sex. They want to rape kids. The Internet can help them facilitate those needs and the Internet allows them to do so in the comfort and privacy of their own homes.

Let's get one thing straight right now. A child who has no computer or access to the Internet still has a great deal to fear from being sexually assaulted. Statistically speaking though a child molester is actually 90% more likely to be a close, "trusted" friend or family member. That is why you should always be cautious of people who want to spend a great deal of time with your child. On the other hand, while on the Internet, the opposite is true. The Internet molester is most likely a stranger. He is also most likely male. He is likely going to try and slowly introduce himself into your child's life and make their life his and vice versa. He will use Internet tools such as web pages, chat, newsgroups, texting, and email as a way to gain access to your child. This is why I urge you to read the earlier chapters on these topics so that you can be armed with the same type of information and techniques that the predator is using.

I cannot stress enough that if you supervise your child's online activities, either through constant and consistent monitoring or by using the computer together, your child's chances of being sexually molested by someone that they meet online is very low. Give your child unlimited access to web pages, email, chat, and other online activities and the percentage of risk to your child multiplies tenfold.

From the CyberCop case files:
The Chat Rooms of Baskerville

Once upon a time, I received a tip that a local man was actively approaching local boys in several of the Internet Relay Chat (IRC) rooms and was trying to get them to come over to his house and "party." I began to actively monitor the IRC chat rooms to see if the information I was getting was valid. I hung out (or "lurked" in chat terminology) in some of the chat rooms he frequented. I was posing as a 15-year-old boy at the time. It didn't take very long (about 5 minutes) before my local suspect logged on and almost immediately began trying to start a chat with me. I accepted his invitation to chat and he quickly engaged in sexually explicit correspondence. Every time I tried to steer the conversation back to normal everyday topics that a teenager would be interested in he would immediately go back to wanting to talk with my pretend 15 year old self about sex.

I saved the entire chat correspondence to disk as possible future evidence against him and was simultaneously tracing his Internet location in the event that I needed to arrest him. The suspect then proceeded to offer to send pictures of other 15–year-old boys. He sent me images of a nude, masturbating young man. I immediately notified my local District Attorney's office of the investigation and we proceeded to build a case.

Further investigation revealed that the suspect was a 35-year-old adult male named "Jim." We found large amounts of email and other correspondence involving teenage boys with whom he had been communicating with online. Jim and his attorney later insisted that he was a victim of some unknown computer criminals who must have broken into his computer and who had placed the child porn on his computer while he was on the Internet. As far-fetched as that scenario was, his defense might have worked except for the fact that other child porn images were found outside of the computer, hidden in the back of one of Jim's filing cabinets. He apparently did not have an explanation for how these "computer criminals" might have broken into his house without his knowledge and placed child porn filled CDs in the back of the filing cabinet in his bedroom. Jim later pled guilty to felony possession of child pornography images.

I wish that I could say that this was not a typical case; however, it is so common that it is scary. I can go into the online chat rooms and meet up with an Internet predator virtually any time of the day or night. If you spend any time in the various online chat rooms, people wanting to engage in sexual chat, nude photographs, and even meetings for sexual encounters will undoubtedly approach you (and your kids). The practice is rampant among the participants in the online chat rooms. A good case in point was the time I was asked to participate in a series of local news stories about Internet Predators. The series was named "Web Crawlers."

From the CyberCop case files:
The Web Crawlers

I have worked lots of cases. One of them involved a local man who was using the Internet to download and trade child pornography. His computer evidence indicated that he had been actively trying to develop relationships with several local 15 and 16-year-old high school students online.

As I reviewed his emails it became quite apparent that these teenage girls had no idea that they were actually corresponding with an Internet predator. The suspect wrote them and was able to present himself as a younger, "hip" teen. The girls did a fairly good job of trying not to tell him too much personal information about themselves (full name, address, etc.). Unfortunately as time went on and emails continued to be exchanged, they begin to share small snippets of personal information. By the time I had read a dozen or more of the emails I had enough information to locate which schools the girls went to. Based upon information obtained from the emails, and by asking people at the school, I was able to determine who the girls were. After meeting with the school principal, I sat down with the girls and their parents at a formal interview. During the interview I shocked them by explaining to them that the girls had been corresponding with a man who was currently under arrest for possession and distribution of child pornography. When I asked the girls to explain to me how they met this guy, both girls said they had met the suspect through their personal ads on the Internet.

"Personal ads? What personal ads?" I asked. The girls explained that the newest fad going around was for them and their friends to go online and set up personal ads at online sites such as www.craigslist.org and personals.yahoo.com. These high-school girls would say that they were 18 years old and wanted to trade emails with men. They were doing it just to be "funny." I tried to impress upon them and their parents the kinds of danger they were exposing themselves to.

I assumed these girls were doing this activity

159

from their parent's home computers. I was again shocked when I learned that they actually used the high school's Internet service to update their personal web ads and to send and receive email via free email services such as Hotmail and Yahoo.com. I was equally astonished to find out that the school did not have its own email system and actually encouraged the students to use these free email services. No one at the school monitored or knew about the girls email accounts. The parents were also unaware that their daughters had their own email accounts or access to them during school.

In an effort to try to curb this new trend in dangerous Internet activity I met with one of our local television news stations to present a series of news stories. The idea was to show the dangers of the Internet and the inappropriate use of these online personal ads by students. The idea was a simple one. Show some actual cases that our police department had been involved in and give parents an idea of just what they should be afraid of on the Internet. We decided to re-create the personal ads that our two high school students had made and show the television audience the dangers of this kind of activity.

After taping the basic segments for the first part of the program, I showed the news director and his crew how to set up the online personal ad. We created an account using a fake name and email address. We then picked an online classified ad web site. We pretended that we were an 18 year old girl and that our intentions were to chat and email with men. The news crew and I decided that we would check back the next day for responses. When we logged into our email account the next day there were over twenty different responses from men both from inside and out of the state. Within 4 days our fake eighteen year old female personae had received over 85 different email messages from men. Several of the messages appeared to be genuine personals from men who were looking to simply chat and email with us. The vast majority of the responses that we received were from men who had only one thing on their minds... sex. They sent sexually explicit emails and some sent unsolicited nude photographs of themselves.

One person in particular, a local man using the email name of "BigBob," was very interested in meeting and having "a good time." BigBob indicated that he lived nearby and wrote that he wanted to have sexual relations with the 18-year-old. The crew and I wrote back and told BigBob that we were actually 16 years old, hoping that by placing the author's age at 16 it would warn BigBob that he was treading on thin ice and needed to back off (the age of sexual consent in our state is 16 years of age). BigBob responded quickly by writing back "give me a call and we can get together."

After obtaining BigBob's telephone number, we arranged for a female news staffer with a young voice to call and arrange a meeting at one of our local shopping malls. We chose the mall's food court as the location for the meeting because there were a lot of people around and we could have officers in place if needed.

This is a perfectly good example of why I tell parents never to allow their kids to rendezvous with someone that they have met on the Internet. BigBob tried to convince the staff member to meet him at a darkened movie theatre. We insisted on the Mall location. When I arrived in plain clothes along with the undercover news crew, we discovered that BigBob was so excited to meet his young date that he was there a half hour early.

I quickly took a position behind BigBob as he approached the female news staffer pretending to be our "victim."

Girl: Hi. Nice to meet you.

BigBob: Nice to meet you too.
          How much time do
          you have this afternoon?

Girl: Not a whole lot.

BigBob: Would you like to go to the movies?

Their conversation continues, as they talk to each other about computers and of all things, church.

Girl: So it's not weird to you that I'm sixteen?

BigBob: No, Not weird, Not really.

Girl: That's cool.

BigBob: I enjoy the company of younger women.
Have you ever had an intimate encounter?

Girl: umm...

BigBob: Have you ever been with a man before?

Girl: no.

As he spoke to the victim, he began to lean over the table in an attempt to get closer to her. Earlier I had given her directions that if at any time she felt uncomfortable or if he tried to do anything that she felt was inappropriate, she was to stand up and walk toward me. I would then position myself between her and BigBob and escort her to a safe location. It didn't take long before she excused herself to "get a soda" and I followed her away from the scene.

When I circled back behind BigBob the news director approached BigBob and introduced himself. BigBob was quite surprised to see the newsman. However, I was the one who was surprised when BigBob agreed to talk on camera. The man that met us online and in real life turned out to be a 54-year-old man who had just come from church.

News Director: Have you ever done this before?

BigBob: Umm, umm, no I haven't. She is the first person I've ever met off the Internet. It probably sounds trite, but my thoughts of meeting with her today were to convince her that this was not a good thing.

News Director: I have to tell you from reading your email messages, that's hard to believe.

BigBob: Yeah. It's a lot easier to talk the talk than it is to walk the walk. To see this happen on TV and to see it broadcast to the attention of parents that their kids are out there doing this sort of thing. Not everybody out there has a conscience.

News Director: People are going to look at you and say that you don't have a conscience.

BigBob: That's possible and well, it's one of those things... which direction would it have gone from here? It's only in people's mind which direction it would have gone.

News Director: I think you are in a little bit of denial here. I don't think that's where this was going.

BigBob: Well, and again... you know...you can think that if you so desire, you know, that's ok you know, but ah...

News Director: I don't think you're sure.

BigBob: I don't think I would have walked the walk. I don't think I would have gone all the way.

News Director: A 56-year-old man, even trying to meet a 16 year old girl. You just came from church. The irony has to strike you just as much as it strikes me.

BigBob: Yeah. It does... the irony of it all. Meeting here and all. What was the reason for it?

News Director: Do you have an answer?

BigBob: No. I don't.

News Director: You don't expect us to believe that you were attempting to turn her life around?

BigBob: No. I don't. Why would anyone expect that? Would I if I thought I could? Yeah. Maybe I've got a Jekyll and Hyde attitude.

As a police officer, I'm quite used to being lied to. I'm not sure if the news director conducting the interview of BigBob was quite as comfortable with having to deal with being told such "tall tales." This interview is one that I regularly show to parents when I give talks about Internet child safety. Hearing BigBob tell the reporter that he was really only there to "warn" our victim and that he would have never "walked the walk" with her always makes an impact on those who watch it.

Signs your child may be at risk

How do you tell if your child is involved with someone online that you are not aware of? We recently had a case that involved a 16-year-old girl who developed an online relationship with a 28-year-old man from England. The girl's mother did not realize that her daughter had a cyber-boyfriend and that he was on his way to see her until it was almost too late. One of the daughter's friends was bright enough to realize this was a potentially dangerous situation and smart enough to warn the girl's family before he arrived. Needless to say I had a conversation with the guy upon his arrival and he flew back to England empty handed.

Are your kids using the computer when you are unaware?

Check to see if your child is spending time online when you are not aware of it. Are they spending time on the Internet when you are still at work and they are home from school? Are they staying up late at night and using the Internet? Check with your Internet Service Provider (ISP) and ask for a copy of your Internet account logs and Internet Usage. Check your computer to see if files have been accessed or created during times when your child should not be on the computer (see chapter, "Searching for files").

Another thing to look for is suspicious activity on or around the computer. Since you have already taken my advice and removed the computer and Internet from your child's bedroom (you have haven't you?), you should now be able to observe your child while online from the family room, living room or other common area that has been designated for the computer. Be on the lookout for any suspicious activity from your child when you walk by or enter the room. By suspicious I mean they quickly close down the computer software they were operating, they unplug the telephone, they switch off the computer monitor or maybe they turn the computer completely off. I had a fellow detective ask me one day what I believed it meant when a friend of hers stopped by her house one afternoon while her son was on the computer. When the friend walked in, her son immediately began to start turning off the computer and the computer's monitor. I told her that he was doing something on the computer that he shouldn't be doing and to do a search of the computer files. She did and when she confronted him, he admitted going to adult web sites and looking at adult pornography.

Are your kids being sent pornography?

While you are checking your computer and cellular telephone for files that have been accessed, look for photographs and images that your child may have been downloading or that may have been sent by someone else. Using the search function of your computer, search for pornography photographs (see below *Searching for Files*).

Adult and child pornography images are often sent to kids to shock, entice, and to break down their defenses in a method known as "grooming." The photographs are meant to feed children's curiosity for things that are "forbidden" such as sex. The predator wishes to teach kids that sexual activities with other children and adults are "normal" and "acceptable" and will often use sexual cartoons and child pornography images. Sending these types of pornographic images to children is a step in the ongoing process of grooming the victim.

These pornographic images are often sent via email or during chat sessions with the child. These computer photographs are often saved on the computer hard disk drive, and removable media such as removable USB drives or discs (CDs and DVDs). The images are often named with a three letter extension such as .jpg or JPEG (Joint Photographic Experts Group), .gif (Graphics Interchange Format), .bmp (Bitmap) and .tif or TIFF (Tag Image File Format). JPEG (.jpg) and GIF (.gif) are two of the most common graphic files used on the Internet. To search for graphic images, use the Windows search or find feature and search for computer image files with the file names of .jpg, .gif.

Other things to look for

Some other "low tech" things that you need to be aware of if your child is being groomed by a predator (online or not) includes your children receiving packages, letters or other inappropriate presents from someone that you do not know. Gifts are one of the predator's favorite weapons. Gifts can tell kids that they are liked, appreciated, and loved by others and the predator knows this. He will also use gifts as a way of creating some "credit" with the child, repayable at some later date. The items given can also be a sign that the predator is paying the child to keep a secret about something. Cell phones are now one of the more common gifts that predators are sending to their victims during the grooming process.

If you find items that you or your family did not give your child ask them where they received such items. If you do not like the answers, play detective and investigate the origin and purpose for the gifts.

Be prepared to be on the lookout for telephone calls from adults whom you do not know. These calls may occur anytime during the day or late at night. Check your telephone bill regularly. Make sure that you know what calls were made and to whom. Any calls late at night or to numbers that you do not recognize should be investigated further. Consider getting caller ID for your telephone number and begin regular monitoring of the telephone numbers that call your child's phone or home telephone number.

What if your child is being groomed by a Predator

Talk with your child about your concerns and speak with them about the inherent dangers of sexual predators. Tell your children that they need to tell you if someone approaches them online or in real life.

Search your child's computer for evidence of whom they are communicating with. Check their computer email, check their web browser history files, check their cookie folder, check for pictures that have been sent to them, or any other suspicious use of the computer. If your child is being approached by a sexual predator and they have not told you about incident, it is your responsibility to protect your children and to do what you need to make sure that your child is not harmed.

Talk with the police about the matter, even if you do not believe that your child has been molested. In most states it is a crime to simply attempt a sexual assault of a minor and some far thinking legislatures have enacted laws simply making communication with a child for sexual purposes a crime as well. The police can also check the criminal history of known child sexual offenders. It never hurts to ask; after all it's the safety and wellbeing of your child that we are talking about here.

Searching for Files

When you or your children use a computer hundreds of individual computer files are created or modified in some way on your computer's hard disk drive. These files can reside almost anywhere on the hard disk drive. Your child can also have placed files in areas of the hard drive that they don't want you to see. You need to know how to go about finding these files. Most computer operating systems (OS), including the popular Microsoft Windows, has the built in ability to search your computer hard disk drive and other computer media for files that have been stored there.

In the newer Microsoft Windows operating systems, you can use the search function located under the Windows Start Menu icon in the lower left hand corner of the Windows desktop. Using the search function you can locate files by name, date, size, location, or even search the computer for specific words or phrases (Figure 45).

Figure 45

Searching for Internet Images

In this example we are going to look for computer Internet images (jpg and gif format). Locating computer images will give you an idea of the types of images that your kids are looking at.

Begin by going to the "Start" button located in the lower left-hand corner of your Windows computer screen. Once you have selected the Search box, you simply enter the name of the file(s) that you are looking for. These are most likely in the form of a file name plus a three-letter extension. Some examples would be "playboypic.jpg" or "sex.gif." Since we are looking for computer images, let's ask the computer to present us with a list of images with the extensions of .jpg (JPEG) and .gif (GIF). We will also add to our search request what is called a "wild character" represented as an asterisk (*). Adding the wild character will tell the computer to find all .jpg and .gif files no matter what the first part of the name is. We should do this because computer file names, especially graphic images and photographs, may be named one thing but can contain something quite different.

To search for all jpg and gif images on your main computer hard disk drive using Windows Vista or Windows 7, enter the following into the search term in the Windows search box and press the "Enter" key to begin the search (Figure 46).

Figure 46

The results will appear in a new dialog box. Depending on the size of your computer's hard disk drive this may take a few minutes.

Once the computer has located the graphic files it will present you with a list of the files that it found (Figure 47). Your search may result in a very large number of graphic files from your hard disk drive. This is especially true if you and your family have installed a number of photographs from a digital camera, game programs, or if you surf the World Wide Web quite a bit.

171

IMG_2090		Type: JPEG image Dimensions: 3456 x 2304	Date taken: 11/28/2004 10:52 PM Size: 2.75 MB
IMG_2088		Type: JPEG image Dimensions: 3456 x 2304	Date taken: 11/28/2004 10:52 PM Size: 2.66 MB
IMG_2087		Type: JPEG image Dimensions: 3456 x 2304	Date taken: 11/28/2004 10:51 PM Size: 2.55 MB
IMG_2097		Type: JPEG image Dimensions: 3456 x 2304	Date taken: 11/28/2004 11:53 PM Size: 2.60 MB
IMG_2095		Type: JPEG image Dimensions: 3456 x 2304	Date taken: 11/28/2004 11:52 PM Size: 2.59 MB
IMG_2094		Type: JPEG image Dimensions: 3456 x 2304	Date taken: 11/28/2004 11:51 PM Size: 2.68 MB
IMG_2093		Type: JPEG image Dimensions: 3456 x 2304	Date taken: 11/28/2004 11:50 PM Size: 2.60 MB
IMG_2092		Type: JPEG image Dimensions: 3456 x 2304	Date taken: 11/28/2004 11:49 PM Size: 2.62 MB
IMG_2091		Type: JPEG image Dimensions: 3456 x 2304	Date taken: 11/28/2004 11:48 PM Size: 2.57 MB
IMG_2086		Type: JPEG image Dimensions: 3456 x 2304	Date taken: 11/28/2004 10:38 PM Size: 2.73 MB
IMG_2085		Type: JPEG image Dimensions: 3456 x 2304	Date taken: 11/28/2004 10:36 PM Size: 2.90 MB
IMG_2084		Type: JPEG image Dimensions: 3456 x 2304	Date taken: 11/28/2004 10:34 PM Size: 2.71 MB

Figure 47

One trick is to look for picture files that are large, such as those that are over 10k (kilobyte) in size. Another technique is to look for images that have been modified on those days when you believe that your child is using the computer, such as dates and times after school hours or late at night. You can also sort this list by clicking on each of the titles at the top of the list (Name, In Folder, Size, Type, or Modified). For example, if you want to look at only the largest pictures first, then click on the title that says "Size". Clicking once on the "Size" bar will first sort the list by the smallest images down to the largest. Click on the "Size" bar again and it will resort the list with the largest images appearing first.

To view a particular image in Windows, double click or right click and choose "Preview" to view the file. Windows will then open the image up in any one of a number of graphic image viewing programs (such as Windows Photo Viewer).

With the search function you can get even more specific searches depending on what kinds of clues you are looking for. You could search for all .jpg images and then you can narrow your search for files that were created on a specific date.

Searching for files by Date

When computer files are created or altered, the time and date of the change is written by the operating system onto an area of the computer hard disk drive. If the computer is not used or was off at the time there should be no files with a time and date during the period when the equipment was off.

To check your computer for times when your kids should not be using the Internet, you first need to check your computer's time and date function to make sure that it is accurate. If the computer's internal clock is not accurate, then the files contained on the computer may not have accurate times and dates associated with them. If you can't trust the computer's clock then you cannot trust the results of your searches. To check your computer's time and date, look at the clock in the lower right hand side of your Windows computer and confirm that the time displayed is accurate (Figure 48). You can also place the computer's pointer over the clock for the current date.

Figure 48

You can even click on the time and get the "Time/Date Properties" dialog box (Figure 49).

173

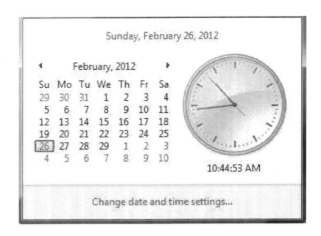

Figure 49

Once you have confirmed that the computer's time and date are accurate, you can proceed to the search function.

To search for files based on a date using the Windows 7 operating system, go to the "Start" button usually located in the lower left-hand corner of the Windows desktop screen and enter the following into the search bar (Figure 50):

Type:=.jpg datecreated:2/11/12

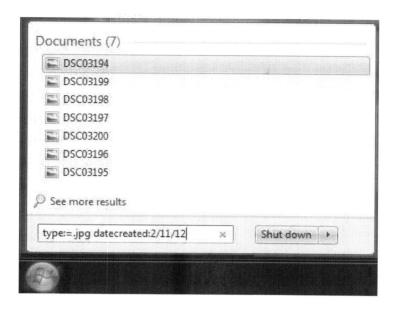

Figure 50

Those jpeg images that were saved, or created on 2/12/2012 will appear above your search term.

With the Windows 7 search function you can search for all jpegs created on a date (as show above) or you can use other variables such as:

Type:=.jpg datecreated:today
Type:=.jpg datecreated:yesterday

If nobody was supposed to be using the computer during that period of time and the computer clock is correct, it is as Ricky Ricardo used to say, "Lucy, you have some splaining to do!" (see also "From the CyberCop Case Files: Best Friends and Worst Enemies")

The Windows search function can also be a valuable tool in

175

searching your computer for specific files or even particular words that are located in those files. I use the search function to look for specific names and keywords that are important to a particular case that I might be working on. For example, I had a case where the suspect was accused of attempting to murder his entire family. Using the search function and a series of keywords that were relevant to the case, I was able to locate files that contained his motive and the apparent timeline for the murders. I don't expect that you as parents are going to need to look for homicide evidence on your home computer (at least I hope not). I do want to stress that the search function can be a valuable tool for you to use in looking into the activities of your children when they use the computer and the Internet. Best of all the search functions are free and with a little practice it is a great tool for parents to have.

From the CyberCop case files:
The Case of the Happyman

The U.S. Customs and Border Protection is most famous for its tremendous and diligent work at protecting the United States and our borders from illegal smuggling, which includes drugs, weapons and even child pornography (for more information about the U.S. Customs and Border Protection, visit their web site at: www.cbp.gov). Once upon a time, a Resident Agent at our Customs office told me that they had a case involving the distribution of child pornography and wanted to talk with me about the computer aspect of the case. Child pornography is photographic images, either in printed or electronic form, that clearly depict children under the age of 18 years of age and who are shown in the images to be engaging in sexual activity.

The agent reported they had recently received information from the U.S. Customs Bureau in Honolulu, Hawaii and in Indianapolis, Indiana about a series of child pornography images. U.S. Customs in Indiana had a suspect in custody for the sexual assault of a juvenile female and had evidence that he had been actively trading child porn with an unknown male adult somewhere in Alaska. The Indianapolis bureau sent the Anchorage office copies of emails between the two men. I was asked to take a look and see what I could discover about our possible suspect here. The emails were almost a year old when I received them. I took them back to my office and tried to see what I could learn from them.

The first thing I did was look at the email headers to see where the emails might have originated from. According to the emails, our suspect was located somewhere in Alaska and he was using the email address of happyman@alaska.net. I recognized the email address for Happyman as one that was managed by one of our larger Internet Service Providers (ISP) Internet Alaska. I went to the ISP's web site and to several different search engines (Google, Bing, Yahoo!, etc.) to begin searching for signs of our Happyman suspect. Within a few minutes I was able to learn that Happyman was most likely a 40-year-old adult male who lived in a town not far from me. I was able to obtain a possible name and address to his residence. Happyman also had a series of web pages. I immediately became convinced that this was the person that U.S. Customs was looking for. Happyman's web pages were a window into his cyber world. While they did not contain images of child pornography, he had what is best described as a "slant" or obsession and attraction to female children. His web pages were described by him in the following terms:

"Dedicated to the most beautiful people on Earth!" and "My site is designed for the sole purpose of pleasing your eyes and ears!"

Happyman had areas of his web site devoted to some of his favorite subjects: young girls, including an area created referencing children's clothing and child models from an Italian Fashion magazine called Vogue Bambini. Happyman wrote, "I highly recommend it [Vogue Bambini] for kid lovers of all ages!"

When you see phrases such as "kid lover," or "boy" or "girl lover" these are phrases that you need to be highly suspicious of. These are the types of phrases that Internet Predators use when they are talking or writing about their sexual preference for children (they tend to use words like "sensual" rather than "sexual" as it makes them feel that they're not hurting kids rather teaching them about "love").

Happyman also had an area dedicated to a large number of photographs taken from a Spanish-speaking television show called "Los Tigritos." The program was a variety show featuring a cast of Spanish-speaking children; he had placed photos on his web site that featured the young girls on the show.

Armed with this information I headed over to the Customs office to drop off the evidence and we developed a plan to obtain a search warrant for Happyman's home and computers.

While the Customs investigators began to prepare search warrants to bring before a judge, I monitored changes to Happyman's web site. After several weeks, it became obvious that Happyman was a pretty busy guy. Every few days he would place new photographs of girls from Vogue Bambini magazine and he would put up new images from the Los Tigritos television show. Several of the images he claimed to have gotten from his buddy "Mike." I traced Mike's email account back to a man in New Jersey. When U.S. Customs ran a check on Happyman's friend Mike, we learned that Mike had a past history of receiving child pornography.

During the month it took to get everything in place, I sought regular updates from Happyman's web site, only to discover an extremely scary situation. Happyman apparently was no longer happy with other people's photographs of young girls. He was now advertising on his web site his own in-home photography studio and he was posting some of the images of children that he himself had taken! Although all of the girls were clothed, the photos showed images of girls approximately 5 to 16 years of age in different styles of clothes, including bathing suits. Happyman named his new business "My Imaging" and described his site as:

"My Imaging was created to showcase and promote the most beautiful people on Earth ... our children. All of the images shown on this page were shot in my home studio, and all models brought their own personality - which I did my best to capture. These kids represent our future, and they enhance our present. Their beauty is direct, pure, and unencumbered by the burdens of adulthood. If you would like to hire any of these models for a photo session, or use any of these images for publication, please contact me."

When this new information was brought to the attention of U.S. Customs investigators, they stepped up the criminal process and obtained a search warrant for Happyman's house. The plan was to speak with Happyman at his office and away from his home. We wanted to hear what he had to say and to give him an opportunity to give us an explanation for his online activities before searching his house.

The Resident Agent for U.S. Customs and I interviewed Happyman while the rest of our team waited for the word to enter his house. We entered Happyman's office that morning and introduced ourselves as law enforcement investigators. While Happyman appeared quite shaken at our request to speak with him, we began with simple questions. As the conversation moved to computer subject matter, Happyman's left hand began to shake. He continuously drank from a cup, even once it was emptied.

We asked him about his Internet email address (happyman@alaska.net) and could he help us in understanding exactly who this "happyman" guy was? He smiled and said proudly "why I'm Happyman!"

When we asked him about the suspect in Indianapolis and the child pornography images that he and another man had traded over the Internet Happyman did not look too happy. He claimed that his memory of the events to be "dim" and he had a difficult time keeping his composure. He denied sending or receiving images of children engaged in sexual acts. He stated that his photography studio was legitimate. He told us that he was recently contracted by a man in England named "Paul" to photograph young girls for a series of children's poetry books. When I asked him if we were to go to his house and look at his computer, would we find images of child pornography, he answered, "I don't think so." I then asked him if he would mind letting us go to his house and look in his computer, he paused and then stated, "Not without a search warrant."

When the Customs Investigator handed Happyman a copy of our search warrant for his house and computer, he leaned forward in his chair, sighed and asked for some aspirin.

At Happyman's residence we located a computer system in the living room along with videotaping equipment. We discovered that Happyman's bedroom had been converted into a makeshift photo studio. We also found hundreds of photographs of local girls who had come to his "studio" for model shoots.

While searching, one of the investigators came across dozens of letters from people all around the country who were asking to buy copies of something called "EyeCandy." Several of the letters contained checks and money orders for this EyeCandy video and often would refer to a place called "TYFLAS." We later found dozens of videotapes marked as "EyeCandy" and "EyeTeen." When we looked at the videotapes they contained hours and hours of video of the young girls at the photo shoots in Happyman's studio. It appeared that Happyman was selling the videotapes of the girl's clothed photo shoots to others, but how was he advertising the tapes, to whom, and most of all why?

As the investigation progressed things became

182

even more bizarre. We located a hidden hard disk drive on Happyman's computer that contained over 8000 images of nude children. If we had to print out all of the illegal photographs, the stack of paper would have been over three feet tall. We also found hundreds of computer photographs of Happyman's models from the photo shoots.

We discovered that Happyman had been advertising in a statewide newspaper for child models. He was looking for girls to model for a poetry book to be made in England. He would pay the girls for the shoot and would give their parents discounts for photo reproductions. Parents would call and set up the photo shoots in his studio. After talking with the parents it became evident that Happyman had developed a convincing scam. He would insist that the parents stay during the photo shoots (at least at first). He told them that he was using the video camera to make sure that he would not miss any good shots of their daughters. In reality we discovered that he was using the video camera to obtain images of the crotch and panty areas of the girls. We also found that quite a bit of the videos contained hours of video images of young girls' feet. This perplexing question was answered when I located the TYFLAS on the Internet.

It turns out that TYFLAS stood for "The Young Foot Lovers Adoration Society" and they are a group of men who are not only sexually attracted to young girls, but are sexually stimulated by images of little girls' feet. TYFLAS maintained a pay-per-view web site, which was operated by man calling himself "Paul." Internet traces of Paul and TYFLAS place them in England. TYFLAS did have a poetry section with content about sexual attraction to little girl's feet. I then discovered that TYFLAS had a section entitled "candy." "Candy" was provided by a gentleman called Happyman. It featured lots of photographs of little girl's feet. The images of our local victims were available on the Internet for download by any Internet predator with a credit card.

These parents had been duped by Happyman into allowing him access to their children while he victimized them unknowingly through the use of video and computer technology that captured inappropriate photographs of the girls without their awareness. Happyman's scam had not been operational but for a couple of weeks before he was served the search warrant. It is clear that we prevented more victimization that would have occurred once Happyman had managed to gain the confidence of the parents and convince them to leave their daughters alone with him.

Happyman was arrested and pleaded guilty to felony possession of child pornography and wire fraud. To this day I still come across photos of Happyman's victims while doing Internet investigations. The images he stole from his victims are forever a part of the Internet. I can never recover nor destroy all of the copies of the photos

> that are out there in cyberspace. These are images
> of a crime in progress and will never go away.
> These images are a moment in time when
> someone who should have been protecting a child
> was instead hurting the child. That is why we must
> all be diligent in protecting our children.

The Internet is here to stay. You can choose to acknowledge it, learn from it, and deal with it, or you can choose to ignore the dangers and deal with it after your child becomes a victim. I strongly suggest that you choose to be as knowledgeable as you can about your child's online activities, before your child is victimized.

I've got some more bleak information for you. You think that having your kids victimized by others while on the Internet is bad, just wait until you find out that your son or daughter is using the Internet and computer technology to victimize other people.

Your child as a perpetrator

There have been many television shows, publications, and articles dealing with the more hideous side of the Internet and the need to protect our children from this dark side of cyberspace (Dateline's To Catch a Predator, etc.). What I see in the many cases that I have been involved with is that alongside this side of the net is also the ability for our children to act out and to take advantage of the power of the Internet in order to commit crimes against other people. Our kids are using online information to teach themselves about unsafe, unhealthy and even criminal activities and they are using the Internet to commit these crimes online and in real life. Our kids are sometimes using technology for bad and not for good.

Is the Internet to blame? Probably not. The Internet is not completely off the hook as it does bear some of the responsibility. The Internet makes acquiring the information and the tools that are instrumental in committing these crimes faster and easier to obtain. It also creates the perception that one can be anonymous online. Using the World Wide Web, search engines, the Newsgroups, chat rooms and email, your kids can find out about every area of criminal activity from how to make bombs to how to steal credit cards.

The ability to use the Internet to reach out and "touch" someone without leaving the comfort of your bedroom is very appealing to some kids (and adults too). At this point I have to reiterate my number one rule for Internet Child Safety is to take that first step and

"Get the Internet out of your child's bedroom."

This is the first step in protecting your child from others as well as from themselves. By allowing your child full and complete access to the Internet you are giving your child a free airplane ticket to anywhere in the cyber world that they want to go and the authorization to do what they want when they get there.

For online perpetrators the computer and the Internet often take the "victims" out of the crimes thus making it easier for young criminals to justify in their minds that they really were not hurting anyone at all. This Internet environment allows kids to "disassociate" themselves from their crime victims. This makes it easier for kids to commit these crimes. Current statistics and my experience say that kids are committing more crimes online. In many cases their crimes will escalate from petty juvenile pranks to major international criminal enterprises with severe civil and criminal penalties.

So if the Internet shares some of the blame, who else is involved in the mix? The kids, of course, do bear quite a bit of the responsibility. Many of the juveniles that I have arrested tell me that they knew what they were doing was wrong and illegal. They did it anyway. Instead of toilet papering a house as we might have done as youngsters, they deface a company's web page or bully someone using a social networking site or text messaging. Instead of shoplifting candy they download pornography. Instead of stealing a car, they steal access to a computer. Unlike juvenile "shenanigans" of yesterday, technology creates an environment where our children can instantly go from a minor infraction to a major criminal activity that can affect people in real life, not just online. The risks that our kids are taking and the consequences of their actions are truly enormous in today's high tech world.

The final piece of this puzzle is us, the parents. We share the responsibility for caring for, raising, and monitoring our children. We also have a part of the responsibility for what our children do while they are online (and in real life too!). Now don't get me wrong- kids can go and do stupid things without their parent's knowledge or consent. Parents can do everything short of locking their kids in their bedrooms (without access to the Internet, of course) and still have their children commit crimes of stupidity.

As parents we have to constantly be on the lookout for clues that our kids are "up to something." It is the game that parents and their kids have been playing with each other for hundreds, if not thousands, of years. I recently found an underground Internet web site that promotes the slogan "it's not a crime to be smarter than your parents." That is a very interesting statement. Kids often begin getting into trouble when they start to believe that they ARE smarter than their parents. In this "Cold War" between parents and their kids, the parents have to arm themselves with information. Information about the Internet and the use of technology is vital to keeping the balance of power on the parental side of the house. Parents need to know what kinds of trouble can be found on the Internet. They need to know what their children will be influenced by. They need to look for the computer warning signs and they have to recognize the clues when they appear. I hope to take the rest of this section and give you some of these tools to help you be better prepared. I give this information to you because, believe me, your kids have these tools already at their disposal, so why shouldn't you have them as well?

CyberBullying and Harassment

As I covered in the section "Your Child as a Victim," the ability to use the Internet to communicate is a double-edged sword. On one hand, the ability to communicate with friends and family is a wonderful thing. On the other hand, the Internet allows people to reach out and trash someone's reputation, to send them harassing or threatening emails, or even to make up web pages that advertise their victim's personal information. All of this can be done with little or no cost to the perpetrator and can be done within minutes of conception to completion, all thanks to the Internet.

I regularly receive telephone calls and police reports on my desk about Internet harassment, stalking and email threats. These kinds of online activities have been given the name "Cyberbullying." In many cases of Cyberbullying it involves kids harassing other kids. I have also had cases of kids threatening adults, including some of their teachers.

From the CyberCop case files:
A lesson in Cyberbullying

I knew from the emails the teacher provided that this guy wasn't going to stop anytime soon. He had in fact increased the number of emails he sent the victim, who was a junior high school teacher.

He was using a computer within the school district and was sending them using America Online and free email systems such as Hotmail. The emails had started 4 months earlier and continued to increase in frequency as well as in the severity of the threats.

At first, the teacher did not report the harassing emails as he thought they would eventually stop whenever the suspect got tired of not receiving a reply (which is often the correct thing to try first). The emails appeared childish, vindictive and often contained misspelled words. The writer would state that the teacher was "gay" and a "pervert." The teacher asked around to see if any of his students knew anything about the emails. He requested assistance from his school district's IT department. They were unable to help as they did not keep log records of individual computers or students. He hoped the emails would stop. They didn't. A month later the shooting at Columbine High School in Littleton, Colorado motivated the victim to get the police involved.

After the news stories about the shootings at Columbine High School, our city and our police department became hyper-sensitive to threats against kids and teachers. That week we received dozens of police reports concerning threatening telephone calls and emails to students and faculty. One report of a bomb threat was investigated and the students who placed the call were charged with a felony for their little "prank." That was around this time that we also got a call about a series of threatening emails to a local Junior High School teacher was receiving.

Our victim reported that he began getting emails from the suspect after the Columbine shootings. The suspect also began to send emails to other teachers and students as well. These emails told the Jr. High teacher's colleagues that he was a "pervert" and likes to "touch his students." They also state that the teacher was going to "get what was coming to him." The tone of the emails were hostile and vindictive. The newest emails were coming from an unknown Internet account.

We began by confirming with the school district's IT department as to the availability of computer log files showing who accessed what computers and when. They informed us that they could not even tell me what school the emails came from, let alone what classroom or which computer sent it. The suspect could be one of the teacher's own students and the school district had no way to know. School district computer personnel said "it is too difficult to implement a logging and password system," which translates into we don't know how, we don't have the money, or we just don't have the time.

Frustrated, but not defeated, I began to trace the email accounts. In order to do so I had to have a search warrant signed by a judge to obtain the records. After obtaining the proper search warrant I then had to send it to the law enforcement coordinator at the ISP and wait. Several days later I had my answer. The account records indicated our suspect was trying to be tricky and hide his tracks. The account belonged to a gentleman in southern California. Our suspect had stolen someone else's Internet account and was using it to send the threatening emails. It appeared that our suspect was into more than just sending nasty emails. He was involved in password and identity theft as well.

With the heightened fear of the possibility of school shootings, students came forward and provided information about the suspect—we had a name. What I needed was physical evidence to put the two pieces together.

I received that last piece of evidence in the form of one of the emails the suspect sent using the free web based email system called Hotmail. By obtaining an IP addresses which led me to a local Internet Service Provider (ISP). The search warrant provided me with an account name and a physical location for the suspect. The name provided by students was a match. He was a 14-year-old boy and a student of the victim.

A search warrant for the residence was obtained and I led the team of investigators into the house while another investigator interviewed the suspect and his parents. In the house we found a computer downstairs near the kid's bedroom. The computer was seized and taken back to our computer crime lab for a complete forensic examination.

At first the student denied any knowledge of the

emails, however; the testimony of his fellow students and the computer log files showing that the emails came from his house were pressure enough. The fourteen year old claimed he had done it only because the teacher did not let him sit at one of his favorite computers. The suspect was asked, "You spent the last four months terrorizing this teacher, sending harassing emails to him, to other faculty, and to other students and you did so because the teacher made you sit at another computer? Is that correct?" He replied "yes sir."

The student was later charged with harassment.

In one particular investigation involving threats via the Internet, what started out as a pair of best friends turned into a case of classmate rivalry. It later ended with a misguided attempt to ruin another person's credibility.

From the CyberCop case files:
Best Friends and Worst Enemies

The April 20th anniversary of the Columbine High School shootings in Littleton, Colorado is always a tense time for parents. The first anniversary seemed especially tough. In our city, as in many cities and towns around the country, people were concerned for their children. In our city half of the parents kept their children home from school after hearing rumors of a possible Columbine-like shooting. At our police department we had extra patrols and officers stationed in nearly every school. We were also sensitive to any threats that came in, whether from the telephone or via email. That week we received a dozen or more complaints about threats to students. Several of the threats came from anonymous Internet sources.

One report was particularly disturbing and I chose to follow it up myself. The report indicated that a 14-year-old high school student named "Megan" and her best friend, "Alice" had gotten into a dispute over a boy at school. The at one time good friends began using intimidation and a series of name-calling during school hours to get back at each other. Eventually they each began sending each other harassing and obnoxious emails.

Their actions caught the attention of the school's administration, which placed both girls on a temporary suspension. A week before the anniversary of the Columbine School Shooting, Megan began receiving emails from Alice. In the emails, Alice used her name and her parents' email account to send Megan messages which contained photographs of guns, blood, and made specific references to having Megan killed at a particular time and place at school. Understandably Megan and her parents brought the emails into the school and demanded that the school do something to ensure the safety of their child. The school contacted the police and the responding officer brought the case to my attention.

The progressive number and increased violence in the content of the emails forced us to quickly begin an investigation into the matter. During an interview, Alice denied any knowledge and refused to take responsibility for the emails. Her demeanor and her responses to questions appeared to be truthful and seemed reliable, however, the police have been lied to before. What we needed to do was trace the email messages back to their source.

Luckily, we had a victim and her parents who were cooperative and willing to help us in the investigation. We were able to obtain the emails header information. The header data revealed that the originating Internet Protocol (IP) number appeared to come from an email provider located in another state. After obtaining a search warrant for the suspect's email address, we were directed to an Internet Service Provider (ISP) located within our area. We now knew that the suspect was nearby and had the accessibility to carry out their threats. A search warrant for the local Internet Service Provider (ISP) was in order. In our search we discovered that the suspect, Alice, and her family did not use the same local Internet Service Provider as the one that had been used to send the threatening emails. In fact, additional interviews by detectives determined that at the exact moment that the email threats were sent to the victim (3:34 p.m.) the suspect was at an outdoor church function. She was seen by some twenty other people, all of whom stated that Alice was outside at the time and was nowhere near a computer or the Internet.

We served the search warrant electronically and waited for the results to be faxed back to us. Twenty minutes later, we received the news that we had already suspected was coming. The account used to send the threatening emails at the date and time in question belonged to the victim's family and was sent from the victim's own residence at 3:34 p.m. Megan had sent the threatening emails to herself.

A meeting was set up with Megan's parents. At first, Megan's father had trouble believing that it was his daughter who had sent the threatening messages to herself. I walked him through the entire investigation and showed him that the email had originated from their house. Megan's dad stated that both his wife and he were at work that day and that Megan's brother was at practice after school. The only person who was at home at that time was Megan. The father still did not want to completely believe that it was his daughter. She had told him that she did not even use the computer that day. I told her dad that if he brought me their home computer I would be able to show him with his own eyes that Megan had been using their computer that afternoon. He agreed and brought us their family computer for examination.

We set up the computer and checked the computer's time and date to insure that it was accurate. I then performed a series of searches over their entire computer hard drive for any files that were created or modified on the date and time in question (3:34 p.m.). If Megan did not use the computer that afternoon there should be no computer files created or changed around 3:30 p.m. Within minutes we had the answer. There were several files created and altered on that day beginning at approximately 3:20 p.m. through 3:45 p.m., all having to do with the computer's web surfing, email and with the Windows operating system profile.

Dad was stoic, but thankful for our efforts. The parents then proceeded to have a long talk with Megan who still proclaimed her innocence until her father explained the trail of evidence she had inadvertently left behind. Megan finally broke down and admitted to sending the threatening emails to herself. She claimed that she did so only because the school did not act like they believed her the last time she reported getting harassing emails from Alice.

This case also shows you why it is important to keep an open mind and to not make assumptions about what might have happened in a particular situation. It would have been very easy to look at the initial information available and draw inaccurate assumptions. Should your child be accused of being a suspect in a crime against someone else you as a parent need to try to be as objective as possible. I will tell you now that it is very difficult for parents to do that. I have had parents yell and scream at me that their kids did nothing wrong or that their kids could not or would not have done such a thing. In each case, the parents failed to stop for a moment and objectively look at the facts of the situation. As a parent, you need to try to separate the responsibility of protecting your child and the need to learn all the facts. You also have a right to insist that a good and thorough investigation be performed. Keep in mind that in many cases no matter how good or thorough, they can't all be solved to everyone's satisfaction (certainly not to my satisfaction either). Keep an open mind, look for the facts and remember that all kids, yours included, are not perfect.

Pornography

Adult Porn Pay Per View

I often have police officers stop me in the hall (usually when I'm going for my required quota of coffee) and ask me about a computer case that they have. The other investigators will often tell me that they recently took a case of a man or a woman who called to report that someone had used their credit cards to buy items on the Internet. When the cardholder contacted the companies who billed their credit card they learned that several of the charges were to Internet sex sites, or what are often called "pay-per-view adult entertainment" sites. The officer will then ask me what I think and what I suggest that they do. "Arrest their teenage son," I told them. "How did you know they have a son?" is often the officer's response. "Easy." I say, "Nine out of ten times the suspect turns out to be the male juvenile in the family. They take mom's or dad's credit card number, go online, and head directly to the adult pornography web sites."

That is one reason why I suggest you check your credit card bank statements regularly. Your kids can and will use your credit card number to pay for adult pornography (and other things) online. The dollar amounts are normally not that large ($9.95 to $19.95 per month) and will often show up as unassuming entries on your monthly credit card bill. Look for any entries that you or your significant other did not make. If you do find a suspicious entry, it is very important that you call the company that billed your credit card and determine the nature of the entry. If you find a fraudulent entry you need to contact your credit card company as soon as possible.

You need to call the company that billed your account for two significant reasons. First, you need to call and cancel the adult web site membership. Most of the pay-per-view sites bill every month. That means that unless you contact them and declare that you wish to have the service discontinued, they will charge your credit card the same amount every month forever. It seems funny how I have trouble trying to get my cell phone or my Internet service to properly bill my credit card every month, but the adult porn sites seem to have no trouble billing unsuspecting parents $19.95 per month for rest of your life.

The other reason to contact the billing service is that you want to have a full accounting of all of the Internet transactions involving your credit card. It is your right to request this information and most Internet billing firms will provide it if you ask. What you need from them is the following information:

The Dates of all Internet Connections: You need to know when the person using your credit card signed up for the service, especially the initial sign up date.

Time of all Connections: You need to know the exact time that the person or persons logged into the account and used your credit card. It is also very important to get from the billing company what time zone they use for their billing purposes. Are the times that they are providing created with Eastern Stand Time (EST), Central Standard Time (CST), Pacific Standard Time (PST), Greenwich Mean Time (GMT), or what? This is very important information as the suspect may not be in the same time zone as you and the police will need this information in order to locate the suspect's specific location.

The Internet Protocol (IP) address for each of the Connections: Most Internet billing companies do or should keep the Internet Protocol (IP) addresses of each person who logs into the account. Get the IP addresses along with the dates and times of the adult web site accesses and you are getting closer to determining who used your credit card. For more information about IP addresses and what they are see the chapter entitled, "What is the Internet?"

With this billing information you can at the very minimum determine if your child is responsible for the credit card transactions. Contact your local Internet Service Provider (ISP) and ask for some assistance. Your ISP keeps records of the connections made with your family's Internet account. They do not keep the actual places that your child went and what they did while online, rather they keep in their records the date and time that your family connected to the Internet and what IP addresses you were assigned during those times. Ask your ISP then to compare your account's IP address to the Internet activity and IP addresses of the suspected credit card thieves. If they match, then you know that someone using your family's Internet account also used your credit card. Your ISP may also be able to tell you where the Internet connection was made from, such as physical address of the connection. I had one case where the father refused to believe that his son used his credit card. He was sure that it had to be a sophisticated computer criminal that was running around the Internet ruining his good credit. When I asked the victim if he recognized a particular phone number, he stated that the number was the telephone number for their family's computer modem line. I informed the parent that the person who used their credit card at "wetbabes.com" had also used the family's personal Internet account. Additionally the account was used right after school at 3:30 p.m. and the caller was using the computer in their house at the time. The son later changed his story and admitted that he used the credit card to go to the adult porn sites.

For the record, I have had cases where a person, unknown to the victim, has stolen and used the victim's credit card without their knowledge or consent. The number of these types of cases is beginning to increase as thefts of online credit cards continue to occur. Many of these types of crimes are still "inside jobs" committed by people who have access to the victim's credit card number and a computer.

For those young men who aren't willing or able to gain access to their parents credit cards, but they still want to visit adult pay per view web sites, there is always the adult password archives. On the Internet there are hundreds of places that cater to the selling and trading of adult web site accounts and passwords. Doing Internet web searches for "porn" and "passwords" can point you in the direction of acquiring several working accounts and passwords to adult pornography. Let's stop here for what I call a "law enforcement moment." It is illegal in most states to possess or use an Internet account and password that does not belong to you. If your kids obtain, possess, or use a password and account that they do not have permission to use then it is a crime. I am sure that you have taught your kids not to steal or not to use someone else's credit card, however, it is also important to educate them about using someone else's account and password. This includes not only adult web sites, but also Internet accounts and passwords into other computer systems.

Free Porn Sites and Fraud

I started getting telephone calls several years ago from upset parents regarding their telephone bills. It seems that some parents around the state were getting huge bills from their telephone provider. They felt that some unknown criminal must have victimized them. What we later discovered was that there were a number of high school students who were passing around a web site address and a password that would allow them to go home and download all of the adult porn that they wanted. All they had to do was go to this web site, use this "secret" password, download the software, and begin obtaining the pornography.

From one of the victims I was able to obtain a copy of this particular software. I learned that the "password" was not so secret and that this software that the boys were downloading was more trouble than it was worth.

The program itself was actually entitled by any number of names; however all of the programs do basically the same thing. They hijack your computer.

Once the juvenile (or sometimes an adult) downloads the program from the Internet he or she runs the software. The program would use small type fonts and a small display window to discourage the user from reading the entire message. The reason that the software author does not want you to read the entire message is that the full text explains that by running this software you are authorizing them to disconnect your computer from the Internet. The program will then use your computer and its modem to re-connect to their adult porn computer through an international long distance carrier who will then charge your telephone bill a staggering $7.43 per minute! This particular software says that it routes the telephone call through Madagascar, although I have seen them try and use other countries such as Chad or Estonia. That is how the parents were getting telephone bills for $1200 or more. This is often called "modem jacking"

The companies that make this software sell it to adult entertainment sites as another way to make money. They see it as another way to allow their customers to pay without having to have a credit card. Others see it as trickery and outright fraud.

Parents need to check their telephone statements very carefully and to investigate any charges that they did not authorize. Be prepared that if a member of your family authorized the charges, some telephone companies have policies to not credit the amounts back to your account for these types of charges.

The other side of the "free" porn sites is that we are seeing a large number of viruses, Trojan horses, and computer worms that are being deposited from these "free" porn sites. Once you go to these sites, you potentially allow your computer and all of your data, including your personal information, user names, passwords, credit card information to be sent out over the internet (you do have anti-virus software on your computer and it's always up to date right?). As you can imagine free often comes with a price.

File Sharing – All the free porn you want

As we talked about in the earlier chapter on File Sharing and BitTorrent the ability to share files on the Internet has gotten easier, cheaper and faster than ever. You can now download all of the music, movies, and pornography that your computer can hold using peer-to-peer file sharing. The important word in this context is the term "sharing". When you use the peer-to-peer networks, your child's intention may be to download pornography however the nature of file sharing is that the files that your son or daughter is receiving are also being shared with other people. That means that they are sending files, including pornography to other people, possibly to other kids who are also file sharing. Sending pornography to other, especially children may be a crime in your jurisdiction.

Like "free" porn sites, many files on the peer-to-peer networks contain nasty viruses that can disrupt your computer or steal your identity so the files that your network is sharing may also add to the infection of other people's computers.

Pornography and Sexual Exploration

The Internet is full of sexually explicit images and your kids can and will access them. If not by using an adult's credit card or stealing an account password, then they can get all of the adult porn that they want free from the newsgroups and web sites. In one of the earlier chapters entitled "Your child as a victim" I asked what affect free access to adult pornography may have on young and developing minds. The answer is not simple nor is it easily answered here and within the scope of this book. What you do need to know is that in the realm of the Internet instead of parents directing what are acceptable stands of decency, Internet predators, adult entertainment sites, and other social forces are influencing how your kids are going to view the world and their own sexuality. You need to know that Internet predators know this and that by providing pornography to their juvenile targets your kids will be much more susceptible and willing to engage in acts that they have seen portrayed in images and videos. It can also give your kids more of a willingness to act out sexually in ways that are inappropriate and possibly criminal.

I am not going to say that by looking at adult pornography it is going to turn your kids into sexual criminals. I will, however, go out on a limb and say that graphic images such as rape, torture, sado-masochistic acts, sexual "fisting," "pissing," and other demeaning and sexually extreme photographs do not create a positive or healthy environment for our children. Watching such imagery will not create a generation that sees character and substance as virtues, rather it reinforces the perception that the opposite sex is something that is to be used, to be controlled, and is to only be used for one's own pleasure.

As a parent, I highly recommend that you take the time to read the chapters on tracking your kids' web activities (See the Chapter entitled "Checking Your Child's Web Activities"). Spend time with your kids online and ask if they have questions about sex and sexuality. They should hear the answers from you rather than going to an Internet Search engine and searching the Internet hoping to find a reliable answer to their questions about sexuality.

Sexting

The advent and wide spread use of the cellular telephone has given us and our children such wonderful opportunities to stay in touch and to communicate in so many ways (see also the earlier chapter on Cell Phones). With so many of our kids using cell phones the ability to also miscommunicate has also never been so easy.

The term "Sexting" (Sex + Texting) was originally used to describe using the text messaging system used to send and receive sexual messages between people using their cell phones. Dirty text messages are certainly a cause for concern for us parents as text messages can be printed out, saved, and even forwarded to other people. Words can hurt and sexual messages that may have started out as a joke between two juveniles can become much more harmful and hurtful after the fact. Words can hurt, but not as much as images and video might. The term "Sexting" now includes the use of Multimedia Messaging Service (MMS). MMS allows images and videos to be sent from one cell phone to another. Since the advent of digital cameras on cell phones the use of phones to take, send, and receive pornography between our children has increased. Just as you need to be aware of the potential for your kids to have pornography on the home computer or laptop, the real possibility exists that your children may receive or even send pornography using their cellular telephones.

Additionally, should your juvenile son or daughter be so bold as to use a digital camera, their cell phone, or computer to send images of themselves nude they may likely be committing the very adult crime of Manufacturing Child Pornography. Child pornography is defined by most states as images of sexual acts or sexual imagery involving any child under the age of 18. So if your child takes such a photograph, even if the image is of them, your son or daughter has created child pornography. If your 15 year old daughter's 16 year old boyfriend takes such images with his cell phone, then he too has created and possessed child pornography. If your child sends such images with their cellular telephone or computer then they may also be committing another serious crime of Distribution of Child Pornography. In the United States Child Pornography is a serious felony for which a person can be sentenced to more than a year in jail and in some cases your child, if convicted, could have to register as a sex offender for the rest of their lives. Unfortunately, some juveniles have been charged (and convicted) of taking and sending such images of themselves or of their minor friends. Many states are trying to catch up and reform the child pornography laws to keep our kids from having to have lifelong consequences for such lapses in judgment; however the, act of Sexting often goes beyond just the legal penalties.

The ramifications of such acts like Sexting is often missed by young adults who don't see Sexting as being anything but a harmless form of sexual expression. It is however much more serious than that. Once images of your children are sent out such images often cannot be removed, deleted, or taken back. As investigators of cyber-crimes against children we often find images of children that started out as "texts" between friends that now reside and are collected on computers belonging to adults who enjoy sexually exploiting children. In addition, the emotional penalties for our kids who are involved in this type of behavior can be overwhelming to their lives and their peer groups.

I know of one parent who took a black ink marker to their teenager's cell phone camera lens in order to disable it from functioning. That may be a bit extreme; rather I suggest that you talk with your children about Sexting. Discuss what it is and that Sexting is not an acceptable use of the cell phones or computer web cameras. Talk about how big of a responsibility it is for them having a cellular phone and what the consequences are for not following the rules of acceptable use. Let them know what Sexting is really all about and how a moment of thoughtlessness can have very serious and long lasting ramifications for them and for you as the parent.

Child Pornography and your kids

Let me say this specifically about child pornography. Despite what you read in the papers and see in the media, child pornography is not "everywhere." Child pornography is a lot like drugs. Can a person get illicit drugs where you live? Probably. Is it on every street corner of the country? No. The comparison is the same with child pornography. A person who wants to buy drugs in this country can get them and so can those people who have a desire for child pornography. You have to know where to go and where to get it. There are some web sites where child porn can be accessed by your kids; however, these sites tend to go up and down depending on how quickly they are noticed by watchful citizens and the police. The two most common methods on the Internet for obtaining child pornography are from peer-to-peer file sharing networks, Internet newsgroups, and from online chat rooms.

The Internet child molester will collect child pornography for themselves and to send to children online. Sending such imagery to kids is one more way that the molester will attempt to shock the child, to manipulate the child, and to lower the child's defenses. I have had molesters who believed that I was a child in a chat room send me child porn images, even within minutes of first chatting. The molesters do so to "test the waters" with a child. If the child backs away, the molester can quickly and quietly disappear back into cyber space and be fairly sure that he will not be followed. If the child does not back away, it is another opportunity for the molester to develop a bond with your child. It is easier and safer for the predator to use the Internet than to hang around the schoolyard with a bag full of candy. Although during one of my search warrants for a home of a child porn suspect, the molester actually came to the front door wearing a t-shirt that read, "Candy from strangers tastes best".

Experts in our Crimes Against Children Unit tell me that they sometimes see the victims of sexual molesters growing up to offend themselves. That is not to say that every victim of molestation is a future victimizer, far from it. It does, however, indicate that children exposed to a sexually unhealthy environment can be negatively affected by what happens to them and by what they see. It is still too early to tell what kind of effects this flood of online pornography or child pornography could have on our children as they grow up. Only time will tell.

From the CyberCop case files:
Child Porn of the Apocalypse

I was working late one night when I got the call. It was the FBI. They had received information from their online undercover operation back in Baltimore, Maryland, codenamed "Innocent Images." Innocent Images was created back in 1995 as a federal response to the growing number of online sexual predators and child pornography cases.

"I think we have a good one here, but I don't understand this Internet stuff" explained the young FBI agent. After hearing his request, I agreed to aid him in his investigation.

The agent provided Internet Chat logs obtained by the Maryland FBI. The logs clearly showed that a suspect with the username of, "Apocalypse," was in the Internet Relay Chat (IRC) system and spending a great deal of time in a chat room called "12-year-old-sex" and "dadndaughtersex." These chat rooms cater to child predators and the trading of child pornography images.

The logs further revealed that the FBI in Baltimore focused upon "Apocalypse" because he was running a computer server dedicated to trading child pornography. A server is both a computer and the computer software which allows sending and receiving computer files to and from other computers on a network. In this case, "Apocalypse" had created a computer file server that allowed anyone else in the chat room to enter his server and receive (or download) and send (or upload) child pornography images via the Internet. These Internet chat servers often work by "trading" which means that the server allows visitors to grab images from it and to provide something in return. In this case, the user had to send or upload images to the server to receive the images that they wanted. The more images they sent the more images that they could receive. The automated system was set up so that the operator does not need to be at the computer, rather they can come back later to find hundreds of new images. When left on for a period of time this server would send and receive thousands of images and videos a day.

The images that the FBI found on "Apocalypse's" server were very specific and very disturbing. The server stated that it was set up to trade only hardcore kiddie porn (child pornography) and was looking for gay and man/boy images. He was specifically looking for images of boys between the ages of 8 and 15 years old. On his computer the FBI located thousands of child pornography images. They were able to obtain a half dozen or so from the server. The images were clearly photographs of male children who were being sexually assaulted and forced to perform sexual acts in front of the camera. There were also child pornography movies available that had been converted to play on a computer.

After running the Internet Protocol (IP) address for Apocalypse's server, we discovered that the agents back east were correct in sending the information to our jurisdiction. The server appeared to be originating within our state. We needed to figure out who owned this IP address and who "Apocalypse" was.

Obtaining search warrants for the Internet Service Provider (ISP) for the suspect's IP address was the first step. Their records showed that the account used by "Apocalypse" was owned by a family located just outside of the city. Our investigation revealed that the family included a male adult, his wife, and several kids including a 15-year-old boy living in the house. Given the nature of the images that "Apocalypse" was trading, we were particularly concerned for the safety of the children given the facts that people who obtain and covet images of child pornography are considered likely to have molested in the past, or are at a higher level of risk for assaulting in the future. The most likely suspect was the father. Although there are some female child molesters, most child predators are male adults.

We began a series of surveillance operations including classified cyber-crime surveillance techniques used to determine the online activity and the location of the suspect's computer. We wanted to know what the pattern of operation was and when the suspect was on the Internet. We discovered that the suspect appeared to be on the Internet 20 hours a day, usually during the nighttime hours. If he had his child porn server running on the Internet, then that would explain the long periods of Internet traffic. We also discovered that the family appeared to be leading a seemingly normal life and regular day-to-day activities. We took the information that we had so far collected and presented it to a judge with a request for a search warrant for the home of the suspect. The judge agreed that there appeared to be crimes being committed at the suspect's residence and that in order to understand the full scope of the situation we had to search the house.

The morning of the search we drove out to the family's residence and knocked on the door. We waited for a few minutes and mother answered the door. We identified ourselves as law enforcement officers and informed her that we had a search warrant for the house which was clean, well-kept and nicely decorated. This was not at all what I was used to. I'm more used to searching houses where there are empty beer bottles, cat urine, crack pipes and garbage throughout. This house had white carpeting and smelled like cinnamon. "This is going to be a cakewalk" I thought.

I asked her where the children were and she said that her eldest son was the only one there. He was upstairs. I went upstairs and knocked on his door. After knocking, I opened the door and identified myself as a police officer to the young man. The first thing that I can recall was the overwhelming stench. The smell coming from the room was horrific. The smell of rotten food and body order gave me a headache. Considering I was only in the doorway and had not even entered the room yet I knew this was going to be a nasty place to search. A young man stirred and sat up in bed. As he did, pieces of old food crumbs fell from his chest and onto the floor. The young man put on his sweat pants and a t-shirt. I told him that I would like to talk and I asked him to follow me out of the room. As he approached I realized that there seemed to be a crunching sound coming from his footsteps as he attempted to navigate across the floor. The floor of the room was filled with trash, including empty soda pop cans, discarded bags of chips, and half eaten plates of unidentifiable rotting food. It was impossible to identify the color of the carpet through all of the garbage.

Another investigator began to conduct an interview with the teen ager, as I put on some heavy-duty latex gloves and went back into his bedroom. After wading through the trash, I found the computer, still on from the night before. I documented the state of the computer and proceeded to seize it. I would conduct a thorough search later at the lab.

The search proved that the identity of the suspect was not the father--"Apocalypse" was in fact the 15-year-old son.

When interviewed, the parents stated that their son had been going through a difficult time in his life. He was questioning his sexuality and feeling depressed, dropping out of school and refusing to go back. He often locked himself in his bedroom and stayed up all night to sleep during the day. His parents did not know what to do.

When I interviewed him the first thing that the boy asked me was, "How did you catch me?" He explained how he had created the chat server himself and that he viewed the photos as an extension of his exploration of his "sexuality." He stated that he was using the computer as an "escape" and that he spent the rest of his time online playing computer games. While he complained that his parents did not understand him, he denied that he had ever sexually molested anyone or that he had ever been victimized himself.

After interviewing the father and clearing him of any criminal activity, it became fairly obvious to all of us there that this family and this child needed some serious help. We worked with state authorities and charged the boy as a juvenile with possession and distribution of child pornography. By formally charging him as a juvenile, it allowed the state to seek out and to provide the family with the help that they would need. It also allowed the boy an opportunity to change his life. If he chose not to seek help he could face disciplinary actions.

Computer Intrusion

We hear about it every day now. Somebody breaks into a computer somewhere and the suspect turns out to be a 15-year-old high school student. Don't think it would ever happen to your child? Think again. I recently spoke to a large group of parents and teachers and I realized that as I spoke to them about how to protect their kids from online predators, I realized that in some sense I was talking to some of the parents of my prime suspects in computer intrusions.

Many kids who become involved in computer break-ins and other illegal computer crimes are bright, seemingly well-adjusted kids. They often get good or above average grades (when they apply themselves). Most of them were using computers before they could walk. They accept the Internet and are curious about it. They are often not challenged enough at school or in their computer classes. They generally don't get into much trouble and appear to be quiet. Like every other kid they are not perfect but few would have ever pegged them for illegally entering a computer network and causing thousands, sometimes millions of dollars in damages and lost productivity.

In today's world your teenager is more likely to be breaking into a computer that doesn't belong to him than stealing a car. Unfortunately, it is the use of the Internet that aids your child in disassociating himself from the reality of the situation. It is much more likely that he will be responsible for committing a felony crime with your home computer than with an automobile.

It's not Hacking, it's burglary

The media has taken the term "hacking" and has made it

something of a misguided term. The media, popular television shows and movies have managed to make the term "hacking" into a "badge of honor" for some kids. The term itself is not about committing crime with a computer (although some misinformed people believe otherwise). The computer term of "hacking" was made popular in the earlier 1980s by author Steven Levy in his book "Hackers." It was a term of technological endearment that was given to technology experts and hobbyists who were able to create or modify existing technology into something else that no one had been able to do, or to do something better with the technology.

As computers and the Internet became common place, the media and some misinformed individuals took early reports of computer criminals that called themselves "hackers" at their word. The name was short, catchy, and easy to spell. The more acceptable and proper computer term for one who breaks into a computer without authority to do so is a "cracker." In my world, someone who is breaking into a place that they are not allowed to be in is an intruder and they are committing the crime of burglary (or more specifically Criminal use of a Computer A.S. 11.46.740).

As parents you need to be able to talk to your kids about computer "cracking" and explain to them that entering someone else's computer without the proper consent is a crime. It is no different than if they broke into someone's house. Just because the house is 4,000 miles away and you went into the residence via the Internet line does not make it any less criminal. The victims of computer intrusions are real people and are often just as victimized as the person who discovered that someone has broken into their home. The law makes it very clear that it is a crime and in many cases you do not even have to enter and do something to the computer to be prosecuted. The act of simply entering an unauthorized computer can bring you to the attention of law enforcement. With the growth, size, and our continuing dependence on the Internet for vital information, goods, and services, the risks are becoming high and the potential for tragedy is too great for us to not take this kind of activity seriously.

Take the time to explain to your kids that this sort of activity is not acceptable. Your kids should learn that they should not break into a computer or network that does not belong to them even out of "curiosity". They should not victimize someone else just as they would not want their own computer to be broken into by someone else.

The problem that we as parents are facing is that although your kids may learn that lesson, it is incredibly easy for them to obtain and utilize the tools that allow them to quickly and easily commit such crimes while on the Internet.

Things that go bump on the net

As technologies like the World Wide Web have made using the Internet as easy to use as pointing at a picture and clicking a mouse, so has the technology made committing online crimes easy to do. It used to be that a computer criminal had to be a computer science major at a university to have the knowledge and tools necessary to break into or interfere with others on the Internet. Unfortunately, for law enforcement and for parents around the world, this is not so anymore. As the technology gets easier to use, so have the tools for committing crimes.

Scanners

There are programs out there now that your kids can download from the internet that will allow them to search a computer system anywhere on the planet for possible vulnerabilities and try to locate ways of illegally entering a computer. This method for scanning a system looking for vulnerable openings is called "scanning" or "port scanning."

Scanning software is available for most computer operating systems and is often free. Scanning software itself has a legitimate use when it is used by a network designer or system administrator for testing his or her computer networks. Network scanners have since been altered or redesigned for more sinister uses. They have also become quite easy to use. Most scanners now have an easy to use graphical interface and are simple to use.

More recently automated software is now available online which will take port scanning to the next level. "Vulnerability Scanner" software can be used to target a specific network or computer and will execute computer code against the target. The Vulnerability Scanner determines what type of computer the target is, and what operating system is installed, and it can exploit known vulnerabilities directly at the target system. Once the system is exploited, the computer or network is completely under the control of the intruder.

Trojan Horses

Like their ancient namesake, computer Trojan horses are computer programs which computer crackers use to obtain access to other people's computers. Trojan horse programs use other software to hide themselves in an attempt to get the victim's computer or their operator to run the Trojan. Once the program is run, the hidden program (the Trojan) begins and proceeds to do the criminal's bidding. These types of programs are available on the Internet and are freely acquired. They are simple to use and extremely powerful. Once installed on a victim's computer the intruder has complete control. The suspect can read all of the files on the victim's computer. He or she can add files, delete files, or make the computer system completely inoperable. They can read your email and obtain your passwords. With this type of software the suspect can even monitor your every keystroke or turn your computer's microphone and video camera on and watch and listen to your every move. All of this can be accomplished by even the youngest and most novice of criminals.

There are hundreds of other Trojan horse programs out there and more and more of them being introduced every day on the Internet.

Using this type of software against another person is a crime and I have the cases to prove it. I also have the victim's statements and experiences to tell me that there are real people being hurt by this kind of activity. The criminal is using a person's own computer against them and there are using it to steal and to terrorize and stalk their victims. The suspect is violating the victim's right to privacy without their knowledge or consent. The victim's feelings of fear and loss of security are just as real as if the suspect had broken into their homes and stolen their personal belongings.

I have investigated juveniles and adults who have used such software to electronically wiretap someone without their knowledge via the Internet. Many of the juveniles that I have interviewed have stated that they knew that it was wrong but they didn't think that they would get caught or they simply stated that they did not understand the ramifications of their actions nor the problems that it would cause.

I had one parent who told me that their child was doing the computer companies a favor by "breaking into the computers". According to the parent, his son was showing them where their computer weaknesses were and was going to help them by telling them how to fix them. I have heard the, "I was trying to help them by breaking into their computer," justification for computer burglary before and it doesn't hold water with me. I asked the father who was in the construction business if he would allow his workers to drive around town and randomly enter other people's houses without the knowledge or consent of the owners. "No," he answered. I then asked him "Would you allow those same workers to then begin inspecting the homes that they illegally entered for areas that required remodeling and begin tearing down sections of the house that they felt needed repair?" The father replied, "No, of course not." "That," I said, "was exactly what your son was doing with other people's computer networks." His son's victims did not ask to have their computers and their private and personal information violated by his son's actions, regardless of what kind of "service" his son may have been trying to provide.

Computer Viruses

Computer viruses are a second cousin to Trojan horses. Computer viruses are usually small computer programs, which are designed to infect a computer. They are often created to cause damage or injury to the victim's computer. Like their real world counterpart, computer viruses will often attempt to replicate themselves and are known to travel from one computer to the next causing additional damage and inconvenience.

Computer viruses can easily be obtained on the Internet by your kids and are a serious and dangerous subject for your children to be playing with. Messing around with live computer viruses is a hazardous thing for anyone, especially for novices. There are computer programs available on the Internet that will allow kids to build their own computer viruses with little or no programming experience.

Like playing with fire, it is easy to get burned by a computer virus. Your kids could easily infect your computer, putting your family's computer system and personal records in jeopardy of being damaged or destroyed. A virus could also easily escape and spread to other people's computers with little or no warning and it would be you and your child who would be responsible for the potential consequences.

Denial of Service Attacks

A popular method of creating havoc on the Internet is the use of Denial of Service or DOS attacks. A DOS attack works on the principal that if you overload a computer with false data or information that is disguised as legitimate network traffic the victim computer or network will soon be unable to deal with the flood of data and will be effectively made unusable for a period of time. This type of attack has been made popular by the many media reports and news stories of computer criminals that have used modified viruses, Trojan horses, and compromised computers to bring down networks belonging to such companies as the Wall Street Journal, Amazon.com, CNN and Etrade. Like their distant cousins, the virus and the Trojan horse, Denial of Service attacks can be obtained and launched from a simple home computer connected to the Internet, but it is more effective when done using multiple compromised computers that are remotely controlled by computer criminals (a Botnet).

Denial of Service attacks are a crime and can result in serious damage to a computer network which can include the loss of revenue as well as the time and resources lost to the victims and their customers. As the old adage goes, "just because you can do it, does not make it right."

From the CyberCop case files:
It's not a Gang,
It's a Club

One day my computer with its built in alarms began lighting up like a Christmas tree. I had been running firewall and virus protection software for some time and was interested in who might be monitoring and scanning my computer while it was connected to the Internet. This time my firewall program alerted me about a scan from an unknown source. The unknown scanner appeared to be scanning hundreds, if not thousands, of computers in my Internet neighborhood looking for a computer without firewalls, or with holes in their security.

Most scans are not disconcerting, in fact, scanning a system on the Internet is not considered illegal, just rude and often suspicious. These scans were consistent and appeared to be performed by a suspect determined to find a vulnerable computer to break into. My analysis of the suspect scans appeared to show that the scans were from a local source. I sent an email complaint to my Internet Service Provider's security administrator. I envisioned perhaps a phone call and that would be the end of the story.

The ISP security administrator contacted me a few days later and shared that my complaint was amongst dozens that he had received from other Internet customers. Our little suspect had apparently upset quite a few people with his rude habit of incessantly scanning other people's computers looking for security breaches. "What do you want me to do about it?" I asked. "Port scanning isn't a crime" I explained. "How about if he actually is breaking into a computer?" The administrator asked. "That is something completely different," I responded, "Tell me more."

The Security Administrator told me that the suspect had accessed computers on the network without the permission of the computer's owner. Additionally, scans of the suspect's own network revealed that he had been busy running a FTP (File Transfer Protocol) server on his computer allowing him to send and receive hundreds of stolen software programs, also known as warez (pronounced wear-z). His computer was filled with hundreds of stolen computer programs worth thousands of dollars as well-known computer cracking and scanning software.

Armed with this new information I launched a formal investigation. Files located on his FTP server indicated that our suspect was not alone when it came to his online criminal activities. He was a member of an organized group of computer users who called themselves the Republic of America (ROA). They appeared to be a collection of computer crackers who were working together to illegally break into computers to steal computer software and credit card numbers (also called "carding"). It appeared that our local computer cracker was an active member of ROA and that they were able to use the Internet to meet and discuss their online activities. He used the name "Flameboy" and was one of four local members. There appeared to be twenty or more members of the ROA scattered around the country. The leader was a man named "LordFox." We learned that ROA was beginning to use encryption to try and hide their illegal activities and to send emails between other members in a secured manner.

After obtaining the physical location of our suspect and his computer, I was granted a search warrant for his residence. We chose to serve the warrant when our suspect was most likely away from the computer to minimize any opportunity for him to destroy computer files. With an entry and search team positioned, the boy's mother answered the door and I identified myself. After briefing the mother as to our reasons for being there she showed us to her son's computer which was located in his bedroom. He was operating a computer and a high-speed cable modem. Flameboy's mom told us that her son used the computer quite a lot and most of his friends were "into" computers as well. She shared that over the past couple of months he was spending quite a bit of time online and his grades were beginning to suffer. She had no idea what he had been up to.

With his mother's assistance we had her son taken from school and brought to the house for an interview. Flameboy was interviewed and he disclosed that he had been using computers for quite some time and he and his friends had been involved in the ROA for the past couple of months. He said that most of the members met through online chat rooms on ICQ. The head of ROA was an 18-year-old who lived in California. They were a group of guys that liked to break into other people's computers and exchange computer software. Flameboy said that LordFox had even sent him some stolen credit card numbers and told him to use them. He refused to use them and had just left them on his computer. When asked why he got involved with this kind of activity, Flameboy told me that he didn't think that any of this was really that wrong but that when someone started talking about credit cards he got a little more concerned about what he was doing. Despite his concerns he still continued his illegal online activities. He also said that he had not thought about the ramifications of entering someone else's computer without their permission.

Flameboy admitted to illegally entering at least six computers using software that he obtained off of the Internet. He stated that LordFox had been emailing and chatting with others in the group about trying to knock out a power grid, possibly somewhere in northern California. When I asked Flameboy about LordFox, he did not really know much about him and was not even sure who he really was. I expressed concern over someone asking members of this "club" to break into computers, stealing and using credit cards, and plan the possible take down of a public power system. As we talked more Flameboy seemed to finally understand the ramifications of his involvement and the potential for serious consequences of his action.

Flameboy was later charged as a juvenile with criminal use of computers, unlawful entry, and credit card theft. I am pleased to report that he has completed his probationary period and by all reports has been able to "keep his nose clean" and stay out of any more trouble while online. He is still in school and has discovered that he enjoys creating computer animation. He is even helping to maintain his school's computer lab. He assists others with their technical computer problems and informs other kids about the dangers of illegal online activities.

Protecting your online family

You can begin the process of protecting your family by making sure that your kids, especially your teenagers, know that you are aware of these types of Internet activities and that these kinds of acts are not acceptable. Becoming involved in computer crime, either as a victim or as a perpetrator, can affect real people and have real consequences. Talk with your kids and let them know that you can be monitoring for these types of activities. If someone tries to convince them that these sorts of Internet activities are alright then they need to know that it is not okay.

I spoke recently with the mother of one of the juveniles that I once arrested for a computer crime. She tells me that there were signs that her child was hiding things from her about his online activities. She now recalls several times when she walked into his room he would act "nervous" and would quickly close down the computer software that he was using. It was suspicious but she felt that she had a good and trusting relationship with her son. She didn't take the time to monitor his computer activities and to move the computer out of his bedroom.

She also said that if there was one thing that she would tell other parents, it would be that "you have to take the time to know about all of the illegal and inappropriate activity that occurs online." She says that as a parent you have to have the knowledge of what is a good use of computers and what is unacceptable or illegal behavior. Once the parent knows and decides what is acceptable they can then pass this knowledge onto their children. Their family had to learn about computer crimes the hard way. She says that catching her son was a good thing in the long run. It taught him that what he was doing was against the law and that he needed to learn that there are others who are affected by his actions.

Check your computer for software that your child may have downloaded and find out what the programs do. Many of the computer scanners, Trojan horses, and virus types of software can come in under many different shapes and forms. If you don't know what a particular piece of software is for, try looking it up on the Internet. Check with your local computer technician, or simply ask your kids where their computer programs came from.

Virus Protection

Get virus protection for all your computers. This is a critical move and every family should have virus protection software running on every computer they own, regardless of whether the computer has Internet access or not. Just as importantly, you must update the virus software's virus definition files regularly- at least every day. Most virus protection software uses a list or a database of known viruses. Each virus that is discovered has a specific data pattern. The software uses the patterns to check them against every piece of software on your computer, as well as all incoming and outgoing information. If the virus software finds a match in its virus database then it can take action and remove the virus before it has an opportunity to infect your machine. Some of the newer protection programs use smart scanning to look for suspicious virus-like activity. The virus definition files are the list of known virus patterns. The problem is that there are hundreds of new strains of computer viruses being written and discovered every week. If you do not have current virus definitions for your computer then you might as well not have virus software running at all. I update my virus definition files at least once (sometimes twice a day) and suggest that others do so as well.

Two of the most popular virus programs are Norton AntiVirus (www.symantec.com) and Mcafee's AntiVirus Plus (www.mcafee.com). Both are reasonably priced and both allow you to automatically get daily virus definition updates. I also use

AVG Internet Security (www.avg.com) and it works very well (AVG even has a free anti-virus only version).

Many of the above anti-virus programs now include additional safety features such as built in firewall protection, (for controlling data coming in and out of the network ports), email and download scanning, online transaction protection and more.

Once installed the software can check your computer for existing viruses as well as scan incoming disks, computer files, and emails for any possible infections. Virus protection software will also alert you if someone attempts to give you a Trojan horse or other types of insidious attacks against you and your family's computer. If you do not have virus software for your family's computer I cannot urge you enough to get it and install it as soon as possible. In this case, an ounce of prevention is most definitely worth a pound of cure. As one parent told me, her yearly virus update fee of a few bucks a year was nothing compared to the potential costs of repairing a computer damaged by a virus.

One of the additional advantages to having current virus protection is that it will help to prevent your kids from getting into or sending out viruses on their own. Your kids would have to disable the virus software in order to use or manipulate strains of viruses and you of course will be checking regularly that the virus software is active and in working order (right? Good.)

Firewall Protection

As I mentioned above, more and more anti-virus programs include additional software to help protect your computer while its connected to the Internet. Firewall software acts like a traffic cop between your computer and the Internet (who says there is never a cop around when you need one?). A firewall monitors incoming and outgoing data traffic between your computer and the Internet.

It will monitor and allow those activities that are acceptable and necessary (surfing the World Wide Web, email, etc.) while at the same time not allowing other activity such as unauthorized computers from trying to enter your computer.

Nearly all of the anti-virus protection software companies mentioned above, McAfee (www.mcafee.com), Norton (www.symantec.com) and AVG (www.avg.com), sell inexpensive firewall software or they include firewalls in their suites of Internet protection packages. You can also try a popular and free firewall program called ZoneAlarm from Checkpoint (www.zonealarm.com). Programs such as these are easy to install and relatively easy to use (always backup your important data first). The first few days that you use the firewall software it may ask you which computer programs that you want to have access to the Internet. You can help teach your firewall software which programs are allowed to have online access and which ones are not. Your firewall software will then monitor incoming and outgoing internet traffic and will not allow suspicious or unauthorized access into your computer. This includes unauthorized entry into your system by computer criminals using known computer intrusion techniques (cracking). Most Internet scanners won't be able to see your computer while it is on the Internet thus making your family's computer a less likely target.

Like virus software I recommend that everyone have both virus and firewall software of some kind running on all of their computers and to keep those programs up-to-date. Having this sort of protection doesn't guarantee that you won't have problems with Internet criminals coming from inside or outside of your home but it sure will reduce the chances of it happening. We have a saying in the Burglary Investigation Unit… burglars are usually lazy and they will look for the easy targets so you need to make sure that your home is more secure than your neighbor's home.

From the CyberCop case files:
The "root" of all Evil

It was a tip from an informant to a local Internet Service Provider (ISP) that lead us on a chase that would take us from one side of the country to the other and then back again. The tipster stated that he had evidence that one of their main computer servers had been broken into and that the system had been compromised at the administrator or "root" level.

Root is the highest level of control allowed on a UNIX/Linux based computer system. When a person has root access on the computer, that person is in complete control of the computer and can make the system do anything he or she wants it to do. These types of computer systems make up the largest number of computer servers on the Internet and are prime targets for computer crackers.

The head of the ISP's Security Team confirmed what the caller had told them. Someone had root level access on several internal computer systems. One of these systems contained accounting information, including possible credit card and private account information.

The system was taken off line from the Internet and examined. It appeared that the intruder had been in the system for at least a month and had obtained root access through a series of buffer-overflow exploits. A buffer-overflow exploit is a technique that takes advantage of the basic structure of computer operating systems and computer software. Software is written and designed to accept and to return information as programmed by an individual or a team of designers. The computer program expects data to be received in one form or another and then will output it as specified in its own code. The problem is when the software encounters data in a form that it never expected or was designed for. Like pouring too much water into a glass there is an overflow of liquid. A computer program can be flooded with data and when that occurs the software can act in ways it was never designed to do such as to allow normally unauthorized commands and computer privileges to be created. This was what the intruder appeared to have done.

The ISP had to assume that other systems might also be compromised and they began the long and tedious process of recreating their system from backups and as a security precaution they began to issue new passwords to many of their users. The company estimated that the extra time and monies spent in repairing the known and unknown damage to their systems at over $10,000.

Like every crime, there are always some traces

left behind. Although the computer intruder was good enough to try to cover his tracks by deleting log files that might have told us information about him, he still had to have some way of entering the system in the first place. In this case, he used an account and password called "johnnyb." Further investigation revealed that the owner of the "johnnyb" account did not appear to have been the one who had broken in. His user name and account password had been stolen and appeared to have been used by others to gain illegal access to the Internet.

With permission from the account holder I began a 24 hour a day monitoring of the johnnyb account.

After only a couple of days of monitoring the account, it became quite evident that this was not going to be an easy arrest. The account was being used by a number of suspects all over town. They were using the account to gain free access to the Internet without the authority or knowledge of the account owner. What began with one suspect now lead us to half a dozen or more potential criminals. I also located and recruited an informant who had access to several illegal cyber-criminal groups.

After analyzing the account activity we narrowed our focus to four locations of repeated illegal Internet access. Using intelligence obtained from many various sources we were able to gather enough evidence to obtain search warrants for three of the suspect's homes where the illegal activities were originating.

While monitoring the suspect's accounts, we discovered that our suspect had learned who our informant was. In an attempt to frighten and discourage the informant from helping us the suspect began launching a series of Denial of Service (DOS) attacks against Internet Chat servers that the informant was working on. The DOS attacks crippled the server's ability to stay online and made them useless. The victim's computers were located in California and were attacked via the Internet from several different locations. One attack was launched by a computer system located in Atlanta, Georgia and the other attack originated from a computer system in Chicago, Illinois. Both computer systems we later discovered had also been compromised, or "rooted" by our suspect. The system administrators for both computer networks in Atlanta and Chicago were contacted and copies of their log files were sent to us to look for any possible leads about our suspect's location or identity.

Two days before Christmas, three teams made up of local police, State Troopers, U.S. Secret Service, and the U.S. Customs office went to the three homes of the known suspects and executed the search warrants. In each of the cases we located computers in or near the bedrooms of the teenage boys who lived at those locations. In one house, we located over eight different computer systems. The computers and the other items located there indicated that each of them had been involved in the theft and use of Internet passwords and user accounts. When questioned none of the suspects appeared to be the ISP intruder that we were originally looking for. They were not able to provide us with enough information as to the exact identity of our suspect; however, one of them did provide us with a name. The name we were looking for was a computer jockey who went by the name "Status." We put the word on the cyber streets of the Internet that we were looking very hard for this guy named "Status."

A couple of days after we served the search warrants the head of ISP security received a strange telephone call. It was a young man who said that he was calling on behalf of Status. Status wanted to talk with the ISP and explain what he had done and that he meant no harm. The head of security told the caller to have Status call him directly and that he would like to speak with him. A few hours later Status called him from a pay phone and said that he was the one who had broken into the ISP and wanted to come clean.

A meeting was set up at the ISP's office. Status was told that he was not going to be placed under arrest but that a Special Agent, the U.S. Secret Service and I would be in attendance. He agreed and he met with us that afternoon.

Status was an unassuming 15-year-old high school kid who looked very nervous as he sat down for our meeting. Status told us that he broke into the ISP's server and had gained root access. He explained what kind of buffer-overflow exploit he had used and how he used it. Under questioning he told us enough that we were convinced that he was telling us the truth and that he was the one who had broken in. He admitted to breaking into the University of Chicago and Atlanta computers and launching the Denial of Service attacks against our informant. He did it because he was "upset" at the informant for ratting him out.

Status admitted to gaining root access to dozens of other computer systems in the state and to hundreds of others across the country. He told us that he liked to break into Internet Service Providers because they had a lot of good computers that he could play with.

We contacted his parents and spoke with them about their son's exploits. We also obtained consent to search his computer system. On his computer we located hundreds of cracking and computer exploits. Status had also collected thousands of password files from some of the largest Internet Service Providers in the country. Many of the companies that I later contacted had trouble believing that someone had stolen the password files to their entire system. One company would not believe me until I faxed them the first few pages of their own password file.

We later learned that Status was also an active member of a group of computer crackers and phone phreakers. They used Internet web pages, chat rooms and computer encryption to carry out their various computer crimes and exploits. Evidence would later show that Status had broken into and compromised well over 1000 computer systems on the Internet.

I also learned that one of the members of Status's cracking group, "Shdwknight," was recently sent to jail for credit card theft, receiving stolen property and for breaking into computers at the Jet Propulsion Laboratory in Pasadena, Stanford University, Harvard, Cornell, UCLA, UC San Diego and Cal State Fullerton.

Status recently agreed with prosecutors to a period of probation, the forfeiture his computer, and to cooperate fully with law enforcement. Status's father has recently been working on the concept of creating a program for young computer enthusiasts that would help provide teens with creative, productive and safe ways to direct their computer skills and talents.

Hate Sites

With everything else out on the Internet to be concerned with you also have to worry about your kids getting into Hate sites, gangs, white supremacist groups, and other racist organizations. With the power and ease of use of the Internet, these organizations have discovered a way to spread their message of hate and bigotry to all the corners of the globe. They can do it cheaply and with tremendous efficiency but using the Internet.

Groups like the Arian Nation, the Ku Klux Klan, SkinHeads, gangs like the Crips, the Bloods, and even terrorist organizations like Al-Qaeda have found that the Internet is a great way to sell their messages of hate. As I talk about earlier in this book, your child can become a victim of these sorts of organizations through their web sites, email messages, newsgroup postings and chat room activities. Your child can also easily become involved in this sort of hateful propaganda and take that step from being a victim to even victimizing others. We have cases of local high school students who have taken the doctrine of hate groups to heart and are actively recruiting other juveniles. They also use the Internet to communicate with each other and to further their positions of hate.

Do these groups have the protection of the right to free speech? Yes, they do. However you, as parents, have the right to control what kind of information your child is being bombarded with especially if the messages are those of hate. As a parent, I strongly suggest that if you suspect your child is becoming involved in such activities, you begin to use some of the tools and techniques found in this book to learn about your child's online activities. Speak with your child and talk about what your family's rules and beliefs are about being tolerant and accepting of others.

Anarchists/Bomb recipes

Want to know how to create a bomb? Want to learn about how to commit crimes? Try the Internet. Take a look at these subjects listed below and see if there is anything that you would want your child to try (Figure 51).

How to make a homemade rocket launcher
How to make a dry ice bomb
Improvised Black Powder
Fertilizer Explosive
Methyl Nitrate Dynamite
How to make Napalm
Making Plastic Explosives from Bleach
How to Make a Landmine
CO2 Bombs
50 caliber explosives
Door Bell Bomb
Credit Card Fraud
Diskette Bombs
Electronic Terrorism
How to Make Dynamite
Nitroglycerin Recipe
Ripping off Change Machines
Mail Box Bombs

Figure 51

This is a small sample of the over 800 bomb files, how-to-commit-crime guides, anarchist, and "black book" recipes that I located on the computer of one of our local 15-year-old suspects. The young man was caught after he set off a series of explosive devices near a local high school. After the boy's arrest the files found on his computer indicated that he was not only downloading and trying the bomb recipes he found on the web, he was preparing to create his own Internet web site designed to distribute the how-to files to others.

Be aware that most of this information itself is not considered illegal to possess (even by your kids). As parents we can however, choose to monitor what kind of information our children are exposed to. We need to be able teach them that the building and possessing of bombs and explosive devices is not only dangerous but it is a crime. It is not the computer file that is to blame although downloading the instruction manual for how to make bombs does not make the situation better. I have spoken with several police bomb technicians who tell me that many of these bomb "recipes" we find on kid's computers are not only inaccurate but some are written with the sole intent of injuring the person who is foolish enough to try and follow the instructions.

Take the time to talk to your kids and explain the obvious and not so obvious dangers associated with this type of material found on the Internet. They need to realize that taking this type of information and actually constructing these types of devices is illegal and that they are putting themselves, their family, and others in extreme danger. Watch what web sites your child is going to and monitor the type of information that they are downloading. Look for hidden USB thumb drives, CDs/DVDs or computer printouts showing this type of activity. It is still the responsibility of parents to be on the lookout for dangers involving their children, not to just be reactive. Today the stakes are simply too great and the potential consequences are too high.

Property Crimes

Just as the Internet has created a brand new wave of crimes that young people can become entangled in there is still a huge number of good old fashioned crimes that we are seeing kids perpetrate while online. Some of these are really just old crimes with a new high tech twist. As the computer and the Internet have allowed us to communicate and crunch numbers faster, the newest technologies can make committing crimes like fraud, theft, and counterfeiting as easy as point and click.

Theft

The computer and the Internet now allow you and your kids to obtain most anything while online. Online shopping web sites and online services such as Amazon (www.amazon.com) and auction sites like Ebay (www.ebay.com) have made electronic commerce (e-commerce) the place to do business. Online shopping and banking is now the place to commit crimes especially crimes involving financial.

Credit Cards

Did you know that there are online groups and chat rooms dedicated to trading and selling credit cards (Figure 52)? You can purchase for very little money one or even hundreds of stolen credit card numbers. The online term for acquiring stolen credit cards is "carding", and stolen credit cards are referred to as "cardz". In these chat rooms and online groups you can obtain various types of credit card numbers that have been stolen from merchants and banks and from around the world. You need to check your monthly credit card bills closely every month.

#CARDER.ORG	5	Talks about carding [+o / +v verr 1] If any @ or +v rips any user then mail the chat logs at founder@
#credit-carding	19	**VV3IC0IVI3 t0 #credit-carding 3INj0l y0UR sT/\Y, u C/\n tR/\D3 oIN the IVI4iIN**
#Fraudcard	22	%% %% %% %% %% Make the most of cc at here's ... Don't Msg Ops For CC, CC will give
#mastercard	46	**Trading Credit Cards on the main channel will** _NOT_ be tolerated, **#mastercard**
#visacard	6	Welcome Back!!! Let's start tradin' shit again, but plz don't do it in the main or u'll get +akick! /msg

Figure 52

Many credit cards are obtained through fraudulent means such as tricking people into giving up their credit card numbers via email, chat, or fake web pages. Your son or daughter can now commit serious credit card fraud using your computer and simple software tools from the Internet. Credit cards can also be grabbed by computer criminals that illegally crack into your computer. Other methods of obtaining credit cards to use online can be as easy as going through the trash of your local department stores and getting the credit card receipts. These stolen cards can then be used online to illegally obtain any goods or services that your child might covet. The most popular ways that kids use stolen credit cards online is to obtain access to adult porn sites and to buy computer games and software.

Your kids can also simply steal your credit card number from your wallet or purse. Since you do not need the actual card while online to make purchases it is just a matter of them getting the information from the card itself in order to use on the Internet.

You and your children should know that possession and use of a credit card or the credit card number itself without the consent of the card's owner is a crime. Even if you do not use the card or card number, possessing it can get you into hot water. Take the time to explain this to your kids, especially your teenagers (you know teenagers; they're the ones that already know everything).

Passwords

Possession of computer passwords is a federal crime and is also considered a crime in most states. The most prized passwords on the Internet these days appear to be passwords to adult web sites and passwords to other people's computer systems. Just as credit cards are traded on the open market in the Internet there are web pages and chat rooms dedicated to the sole purpose of trading passwords (Figure 53).

Figure 53

The sale of and possession of these kinds of passwords is illegal. It is also a crime should your kids decide to actually use the unauthorized passwords to enter a web site or a computer that they have no right to enter (Theft of Services, Computer Intrusion). As I have said before, "just because you can do something, doesn't mean that you should."

From the CyberCop case files:
The Model and the Clue

It was the day after Christmas when the 400 emails were first sent via the Internet. Within minutes each of the emails arrived at the Internet Service Provider (ISP) and sat in each of the victim's email boxes waiting to be opened. One of the people who opened up their email was the Vice President of the ISP. When he read the letter he knew that something very bad was about to happen.

```
subject: ISP Customer Service

Dear Valued Member:

    According to our records, the credit
card payment for your Internet access
account is two weeks late.   The credit
card we have on file presently does not
allow us to automatically bill your
account. If you believe that this message
has been sent to you in error, or wish to
update your billing information, please
visit our customer care page at
http://www.sgbilling.com/

    We are proud to be your Internet
Service Provider and we value your
```

business.

Sincerely,
Doreen Morales
Customer Care Department

The Vice President knew that this had to be a scam. His company did not have any billing problems and they most certainly would not have their customers send them their credit card numbers in such a fashion. Besides that, he did not recall any employee whose name was Doreen Morales. His fears were confirmed when he went to the site www.sgbilling.com. There he found that someone had created a fake billing page that looked exactly like their own web pages. The suspects had even used the same graphics and text to duplicate their own site. The only problem was that this fake site was asking for the customers to enter their names, addresses, credit card information, their Internet account and passwords. Further examination of the fake web site showed that written into the code was a command that sent the victim's credit card information to a number of unknown email accounts.

The Vice President notified his network administrators and his head of security about the scam. The ISP immediately began a series of actions designed to protect their customers. They began by blocking all access to the sgbilling web site by all of their customers thus preventing their customers from being able to see the fake site. They wrote a series of programs to scan their entire email network looking for the fake emails and removing them from the customer's email account. They also studied email log files and determined that 135 customers had already opened and read the fake email. The ISP's personnel notified each of those customers about the scam. Filters were created to scan new incoming emails for similar fake requests. The sgbilling web site was tracked down and was found to be coming from a web hosting company in Vancouver, British Columbia. The Vancouver web-hosting firm shut the site down and provided information about the individual who set up the web site. That information turned out to have been falsified and the credit card used to set up the site had been stolen two weeks earlier from a man in Seattle, Washington.

I was at home enjoying the day off with my family when I got a call from the head of the ISP's Security. He briefed me as to what had transpired over the past couple of hours and I immediately opened up a criminal investigation.

The first order of business was to try and trace the fake email messages back to their origin. The emails that the ISP's customers had received had come from an email server in Spain. We then surmised that the server in Spain had either been broken into (cracked) by the suspect or was misconfigured and allowed emails to be routed through it. The emails had appeared to come to the ISP through Spain; however, they actually appeared to have been sent from an Internet account in

Pasadena, California.

The sgbilling web site in Vancouver had been purchased via the Internet and had been bought using a stolen credit card. Further investigation revealed that the owner of the credit card had been defrauded using an identical scam two weeks earlier. We obtained information that the person who set up the fake web site appeared to be coming from an account near Los Angeles, California.

Meanwhile five local victims of the sgbilling.com scam contacted us to report that their credit cards had been fraudulently used. They indicated that they had received the email message and had unknowingly entered their credit card information into the fake web site. We asked the victims to provide us with a detailed account from their credit card statements. We needed to know what was purchased, when, and where the items were sent. Within weeks we were attempting to track all of the fraudulent purchases. Those leads, however, did not appear to be very promising. Most of the illegal purchases were for computer software, Adult Web sites (online pornography) and Internet domain names (sgbilling.com). All of the software was Internet related programs and all of them had been sent via the Internet. None of the Internet companies could provide us with Internet Protocol (IP) addresses for tracing. The items that were purchased led me to believe that our suspect was most likely a juvenile or a young adult. I also believed that the subject was preparing to commit more crimes by buying more web-sites. We began to electronically monitor those potential sites. Within a couple of weeks one site in particular began to show signs of suspicious Internet activity.

The site we were watching soon began to mirror another legitimate web site. In this case the suspect was not copying another Internet Service Provider's web site. This time he was creating a duplicate copy of a web page belonging to a nude model and actress named Sung Hi Lee. The suspect was systematically creating a web site that looked nearly identical her own commercial web site. Both sites visually looked the same; however, her web site was physically located on a west coast computer in California while his fake site resided on a computer in Georgia. The suspect had also chosen a web site address similar to hers in an attempt to get others to accidentally enter his site instead of hers. It appeared that the suspect was preparing to steal more credit cards from victims who arrived at his site thinking that they were really at her web domain.

Other leads began to take us all over the United States. The more leads we followed the more victims we discovered. We found victims in Illinois, New York, Washington, Alaska, Florida, Alabama, Arkansas, Oklahoma, Oregon, Texas, Mississippi, Massachusetts, Michigan and California. We discovered over eighteen different ISPs in fourteen different states and thousands of possible credit cards stolen.

Our break came when we examined the details of the computer code found in the suspect's fake Sung Hi Lee web site. The suspect had left enough small clues that we were able to trace his activities back to an Internet Service Provider in the area of San Diego, California. I contacted the authorities there who put me in touch with the San Diego High Tech Task Force. The San Diego High Tech Task Force is a group made up of local, state and federal agents devoted to investigating computer and high tech crime in the San Diego area. When I told the FBI agent there of my investigation, we began comparing notes, for they too were working a similar case. It turned out that our cases were related. So related, in fact, that we were able to determine that her suspect and my suspect were two high school students who were working together in tandem committing online crimes all over the country. I provided the task force with my case file and other information that would allow them to proceed against the two juveniles (one was 17, the other 16 years old).

While the task force worked on building arrest warrants and search warrants for the two suspects in San Diego I worked with Internet Security expert, Mike Messick, to try to prevent the two suspects from stealing any more credit cards.

Messick and I began by creating a process where the names of known victims and web sites were compared with lists of millions of other known web site names and addresses. What we got back was a list of some fifty or more possible web sites and web site locations that we believed the suspects would use to steal more credit cards. We then began around the clock electronic monitoring of the suspect web sites for any suspicious activity. If either one of the suspects returned to one of the web sites that we were watching and created a fake web site we would be notified of their activity. It did not take long before we received an alert.

I had just fallen asleep when I was awoken by a text message around 10:30 p.m. Messick's computer system had sent me a text message telling me to check out one of the sites that we were monitoring. I fired up my computer, logged onto the network, and went to the site. What was a blank and empty web page ten minutes earlier was now a web site that looked identical to an Internet Service Provider in Mississippi. I called Mike Messick and we began frantically calling the ISP and Mississippi law enforcement. I eventually convinced a County Sheriff to contact the owner of the ISP. The owner of the ISP called me back and I showed him the fake web site. We also informed him of what the incoming fake emails were going to look like. The ISP soon began receiving fake email messages to their customers' email accounts. The ISP was quickly able to pull the messages out and prevent their customers from visiting the site. Working together we were able to stop the suspects from obtaining any credit cards from the ISP's customers.

For the next two weeks we were alerted to six more fake web sites and were able to successfully alert the ISPs and the local authorities to the impending thefts. The San Diego Task Force soon obtained arrest warrants for both suspects. Both boys were arrested at school and charged with computer and credit card fraud. A search of the boys' homes revealed stolen credit card numbers as well as many of the items that they had illegally purchased online. Personal computers with connections to the Internet were also found in each of the suspect's bedrooms. Both juveniles later pled guilty to the charges.

Counterfeiting

With even the most basic of tools including a computer, a scanner, and a color printer your kids can create incredibly realistic looking counterfeit currency which can be used to steal goods and services from a number of places. The problem with that, of course, is that it is a federal crime to make counterfeit U.S. currency and it is an additional crime to actually use the "funny money" you made to obtain goods and services.

From the CyberCop case files:
Operation Funny Money

I began getting reports from around the city that stores were reporting that counterfeit currencies, mostly twenties, were being used at their checkout counters. The items being bought were electronic goods such as stereos and audio compact discs (CDs) and fast food. We did not get good descriptions of the suspects other than they appeared to be mostly teenagers.

The big break in the case came when a sharp eyed cashier at a local fast food restaurant became suspicious when a group of teenagers went through the drive through and tried to buy $9.00 in food with a $100 bill. The cashier was unable to hold the teens while police responded but she did get a license plate number. The car and driver came back to a local high school student. We were able to identify him and a number of his friends as the ones who were passing out the counterfeit currency.

We were then able to obtain the identity of several teens that had been responsible for actually producing the counterfeit money. It turned out that they would create the money using an old IBM compatible computer and would print the money out on a new inkjet printer that they had recently purchased. The suspects would print out the money and then give it to other students at their school to pass around town with each person getting a cut of the laundered money and the stolen property.

The computer system was seized and examined. What was found was not just currency but the time and dates of their counterfeiting process. After examining the files it became evident that the suspects had begun their life of crime by first scanning one-dollar bills into the computer and doing "test" printouts. Within a week or so they were creating the five and ten dollar bills. Within a month they had moved up to creating the fifty and the one hundred-dollar bills. It was estimated that in a month's time they had created and laundered over $1500 in fake currency and had created a conspiracy with their fellow students to help to launder the money for profit.

The students were later charged as juveniles and admitted to the thefts in connection with the counterfeit currency.

You need to be aware that there are lots of temptations out in the Internet. Some of these tools and techniques are very easy to obtain online but the ramifications of putting to use what you have learned can mean the difference between having some knowledge and committing a crime. Whether you are online or in the "real world" taking something that does not belong to you is theft. Entering a place not open to the public and without permission is a crime. You need to ask your kids to think about what they do online. They have to stop and think, "Would this be okay to do in real life?" If the answer is no, then they shouldn't be doing it online either.

Watch your kid's online activities for suspicious action such as turning off programs or shutting off the computer when you enter the room. Check the computer regularly for signs that they have been learning about things that could get them and others into trouble. Get virus software and update it regularly. Install some firewall software. Learn what the computer laws are in your area. Listen to the lessons learned by others and teach them to your kids.

Protecting your children

We have discussed a number of things that you can do to protect your children while on the Internet. Many of these things do not take lots of money they just require that you learn about the dangers of the Internet and take the time to teach and talk with your kids about these dangers. Along with discussing these things with your children it is important to have rules. Everyone has rules that they have to follow and just as your children have general family rules that you have taught them you should have rules governing the use of the Internet. The following rules should not just be considered for home use but are for everywhere that your kids connect to the Internet.

Setting up rules

The following is a list of some of the items that we have discussed and it is a list of Internet rules that your family should consider adopting into your own personal code of online conduct.

1) Have the computer and all Internet access in an easily accessible and visible area (not their bedroom). This includes cellular telephones with Internet access.

2) Discuss with your children and agree which programs they can use and which areas of the Internet are acceptable. For example:

Acceptable	Not acceptable
Approved Web sites	Any sites not approved
Approved Email accounts	unapproved email accounts
Closely monitored chat	Any other types of chats or chat software

3) Spend time with your children while they are online.

Discuss the places that they go and the things that they do while online.

4) Set limits on the amount of time that your child spends online.

5) Do not provide any personal or private information to anyone on the Internet.

6) Locate and maintain the user name and passwords for all of your family's email accounts.

7) Have your children agree to tell you about anything upsetting or strange that they see or that they are sent online. If they have an experience while online that makes them feel uncomfortable have them report the incident to you or another trusted adult.

8) Report all unacceptable or inappropriate email to your ISP or the ISP of the email's sender.

9) Do not respond to unsolicited or inappropriate emails.

10) If threatened or bullied while online contact your ISP and local law enforcement.

11) Monitor your child's email account and email messages.

12) Talk with your child about his or her online friends.

13) Let your child know that people online are not always as they seem.

14) Never agree to meet someone that you or your child has met online.

15) Discuss the many different dangers associated with the Internet.

16) Teach your child to respect others while online and to respect the property of others.

17) If you choose to use Internet filters you still need to have a set of family rules and guidelines for when the filters fail.

18) Learn your local and state laws governing the Internet and discuss them with your child.

19) Be consistent and fair when enforcing the family's Internet rules.

20) Let your kids know that you love them and that you will support them.

Be prepared for your family rules regarding the Internet to change and grow just as your family changes and grows. As the Internet continues to transform our lives, you have to be able to change right along with it. Every day we are discovering new areas of trouble and concern online and we all are constantly trying to stay one step ahead of the bad guys.

You need to be diligent. Like any good parenting, keeping your kids "Internet safe" is not always going to be fun and is not going to be completely supported by your children. As I was once told "Your children may have a say in a matter, but they might not get a vote." It's a tough job but somebody's got to do it. Your kids can't do it alone and they need your guidance.

Teach your kids that there are forces out on the Internet (and in real life) that will try to take advantage of them. It may come to them subtlety or in a more straightforward type of manipulation. Your kids need to be dedicated to upholding the rules that your family agrees to. You need to make sure that your children understand that they cannot take advantage of others while online and that they need to be respectful of others' rights. Your kids need to know that they can rely on you to help them make the right decisions when it comes to the Internet.

Although I have given you some rules and some techniques that will help you there are no quick or easy answers when trying to keep your children Internet safe. Internet Safety is about understanding the positives and the negatives of the Internet. It is about knowing that trouble is out there and to be watchful for it. Safety is about you as a parent looking for and seeing the warning signs. It's about knowing that your children are in danger of being a victim as well as potentially victimizing others while online. It is about educating your children and giving them the tools that they need to make good decisions about their online activity. It's really all about being a good parent in the real world as well as in the cyber world.

Protecting your Internet Child at School

When it comes to keeping your kids "Internet safe" you can do everything right at home and still have to worry about your children while they are at school. For years everyone assumed that your kids were as safe at school as they were at home. The growing number of school shootings has made us all aware how incorrect that belief was.

Many school systems today are providing more and more teachers and students Internet access. Everywhere you look more and more schools are jumping on the Internet bandwagon. Corporations and governments are throwing around money for equipment and installations alike. Students are being put online in record numbers. That can be a good thing. Problems often occur when you spend money to place this amount of technology into the hands of schools but you fail to give them proper training, policies, and security procedures. Without the proper guidelines and monitoring programs the same technology that is meant to help students instead turns into an object that can hurt them or can become a weapon that is used to hurt others.

Does the school have Internet access?

The first thing that parents can do is figure out if your child's school has Internet access. If they do not have Internet access let your school know that you wish to be notified if the situation changes. Join your child's Parent Teacher Association (PTA) and discuss that you want assurances that before the Internet is established in the schools proper care is taken to ensure that all of the students will be Internet safe.

Do they have an Acceptable Use Policy?

If your school has Internet access you need to know if your child is going to be using the Internet, when and where the Internet access will take place and you need to obtain a copy of the school's Internet policies (also known as an Acceptable Use Policy). If your school does not have an acceptable use policy inform the school that your child will not be allowed to use the Internet until they have such a policy. You can even offer to help them draft one. This policy should include a list of acceptable Internet rules for students and teachers as well as the possible consequences for violating the school's rules. The policy should cover such areas as the World Wide Web, email, cellular telephones, newsgroups, and chat. Each student and parent should also be required to read and sign that they agree with the school's Internet policies before any Internet access can be granted.

Banner Displays

Every time a student accesses the Internet the school's computer system should display a message on the screen which reiterates the school's acceptable use policy. It should remind each student and teacher that their account connection may be logged and that the computer administrators may monitor inappropriate Internet activity.

Tracking user name and passwords

Each child who has access to the Internet at school should be assigned a user name and password. The school should then provide each parent with their child's user name and password. If the school provides an email account or access to a free email service (Hotmail, Yahoo mail, etc.) then those user names and passwords should be provided to the parents as well. In the event of a problem such as a missing student, that information may be extremely valuable in locating the child.

Logging Internet Connections

The school district must also keep a computer log of your child's Internet connections for at least six months. Internet connection logs should include the user name and password used, the number of login attempts, the time, date and the duration of the Internet session. The log report should also contain the specific computer that was used as well as the Internet Protocol (IP) address that your child was assigned during their Internet connection. This information should be made available to parents upon request to the school district. Having connection logs does not mean that the school monitors exactly what each child is doing (although it would be nice). When connection logging does occur, does it leave enough of an electronic trail to allow parents and the school to be able to recreate a time and place when the account was used? This is an important part of your school's Internet safety program and must be in place before something tragic happens. After a situation occurs it is often too late to go back and try to figure out what happened electronically.

Internet filters

If your school chooses to utilize Internet filtering software or a DNS filtering solution like OpenDNS be aware that Internet filtering systems are not 100% effective. Schools, parents, and students need to know that inappropriate items and situations will occur while online. You need to ask your school how it expects to handle these types of situations before they occur. The staff of your school also needs to test the system and to be aware of the system's limitations before allowing it to be used throughout the school system.

If all else fails

If your school is unwilling, or unable to meet these guidelines, then you need to seriously consider not allowing your child to use the Internet while at school. How can you protect your child from dangers online if their school is unable to be as diligent as they need to be? You need to become involved and question the school about their Internet policies and procedures (or lack thereof). Your child's school needs to answer to the parents as to how they will respond if your child is a victim while using the Internet at school. How are they going to determine who is the suspect? How are they going to prove who did what when? How are they going to keep your child from becoming a victim, or a child from using the school's computers to victimize others? These are questions that you as a parent need to get the answers to. If your school district cannot provide good solid answers then it may be that they have to rethink how they conduct online education for their students.

Conclusion

There are no easy answers when it comes to online safety. There is no magic pill or computer software that you can buy that will completely protect your family from seeing the darker side of the Internet. As in real life, you try to protect your children from the many dangers that they will face as they grow up. You teach your kids the rules of the road as best you can and try to guide them through life with education, love, and respect.

Your family needs to know what your rules are and what to expect should those rules be broken. You need to use the tools and techniques that you learned here to verify that your child has not broken those rules or placed them (or others) in danger. Monitoring your child is not the responsibility of the Internet, the World Wide Web, the police, or a $40 piece of computer filtering software. It is your responsibility and it is a job that should not be taken lightly.

The Internet is an excellent parallel to real life. There are wondrous and fascinating things to be found there. The Internet has opened up our eyes to the world and has created a new way to communicate the like of which has never been seen before. Nearly overnight it has created a completely new type of business economy. I believe that for all of the great things that life and the Internet have to offer there are dangers. Just as our parents taught us to look both ways before crossing the street we need to teach our kids that the road to the Internet can be a valuable experience as long as you remember to look both ways before crossing this information super highway that we call the Internet.

Be safe.

Glen Klinkhart

Appendix A - Resources on the World Wide Web

Child Safe Search Engines

> http://www.askkids.com/

> www.google.com/preferences

Child Safety Web Sites

> A Cybercop's guide to Internet Child Safety
> www.cybercopguide.com

> National Center for Missing and Exploited Children
> www.missingkids.org

> Get Net Wise
> www.getnetwise.org

Reporting Online Crime

> To report Online Child Pornography, or the exploitation of children:
> > www.cybertipline.com or call 1-800-843-5678

> To report Online Fraud:
> > http://www.ic3.gov

Appendix B - Glossary of Internet terms for Parents

Acceptable Use Policy   A written policy which outlines and defines the proper use and acceptable actions of people when using a computer or series of computers. This policy should clearly define what acceptable behavior is and what is not. Additionally it should indicate the penalties for violating the written policies.

Adult pay per view   An adult pornography web site which requires payment (usually a credit card) to access the site.

AIM   AOL Instant Messenger (AIM). AIM is a chat, file transfer, and conferencing program originally only available for members of the AOL pay service. AIM now allows any computer users to chat and communicate with others using their Instant Messenger system. (www.aim.com)

Anarchist   Someone who rebels against authority and societal establishments, often by non-peaceful means.

Applet/App   A small computer program often designed for a specific task.

Bandwidth   The capacity of an electronic device to transfer information. The greater the bandwidth, the larger the amount of data that can be sent and/or received.

Banner Ad   An advertisement in the form of a graphic or text display, which appears on world wide web, pages (WWW).

Baud/Bit rate   A unit of speed in which data is transferred.

Bestiality   The sexual practice of using animals to gain sexual gratification.

Binary Boy   A Windows computer program designed to obtain text, graphics, photographs, and movies from the Internet Newsgroups.

Bit   A single unit of computer data (either off or on, or 1 versus a 0).

Blocking/filtering software   A computer program designed to stop unwanted data (web pages, email, photographs, etc.) from being accessed by the computer user.

Blog   Usually a personal web site devoted to a person's own thoughts, comments and/or writings.

BMP   Bit Mapped Picture (Bitmapped Picture) - A graphical picture file format in which each pixel (or dot) is represented by a bit or series of bits. No compression or other space-saving algorithms are used.

Bookmark   A file entry that allows a computer user to easily and quickly access Internet web sites.

Boot   The process of starting a computer by loading an operating system. From the phrase that describes pulling one up from one's "bootstraps".

Botnet   A group of compromised computers on the Internet that are controlled by someone else.

BPS (Bits per second) The number or speed in which bits (0s and 1s) which can be moved from other place to another. A measurement of binary data transfer.

Browser	A computer program which allows a computer user to access the World Wide Web (WWW) pages on the Internet. The browser programs (Internet Explorer, Firefox, Opera, etc.) can read and display the Hypertext markup language (HTML) and display the web pages on the computer screen.
Buddy list	A list of internet chat friends. Using a buddy list, a computer user can be notified of when your friends come online, and allows the user to quickly and easily chat with them. First made popular with AOL's Instant Messenger system.
Buffer overflow exploit	A technique used by crackers to break into computers by overloading the internal memory buffers of the target machine, resulting in unauthorized access to the attacker.
Bulletin Board Service (BBS)	A specific computer system accessed by computer users via telephone, or Internet connection. BBSs were first made popular before the wide spread use of the world wide web. BBSs are often accessed by non-traditional means (Telnet, direct dialup, etc.)
Byte	A series of 8 binary units (1s or 0s) which together represent a single character (alphabet, numeric, or a symbol). 8 bits make a byte.
Cable modem	A high speed internet connection device that utilizes the cable system in order to access the Internet.
Cache	A temporary storage area used by computer operation systems and computer programs.
CallerID	The originating number or location of an electronic device such as a telephone.
Carding, cardz	The Illegal acquisition, possession, trading and

methods used of credit card numbers.

CD-R and CD-RW   A recordable (R) and re-writable (RW) compact disc.

CD-ROM   Compact Disk Read Only Memory. An electronic media, a disc, which can contain as much as 650 megabytes of information. Also called a compact disk (CD)

CDSL/DSL   A high-speed internet access method which utilizes standard telephone wires.

Cell phone   A small mobile telephone with uses cellular radio to receive and transmit voice and data over the airwaves.

Chat   Electronic Communication between two or more people in real-time using computers which are networked together. Originally limited to typing messages on a computer screen, however chat can now include voice and video communication.

Chat room   An Internet connection between two or more people who are involved in chat. Chat rooms can take place in public rooms or in private rooms with the participants all connected via computer networks.

Child pornography   Images or movies which depict juveniles clearly under the age of 18 engaged in lewd acts or sexual activity alone or with others.

Ciphertext   The unreadable form of data that is produced by the encryption process.

Client   A computer or computer program which has to connect to another computer (called a server) in order to communicate.

Compact disc (CD)   Compact Disk. An electronic media, a disc, which can contain as much as 650 megabytes of information. Also called a CD-ROM.

Computer Intrusion   The act of accessing a computer, computer system, or a computer network that a person is not authorized to access.

Cookie   A small file left on your computer during a session on the World Wide Web (WWW). A cookie stores information about your visit to a site as well as other information that the web sites you visit have deemed important enough to save on your computer.

Counterfeiting   The illegal manufacture of currency, mostly notably U.S. Dollars.

Crack   The act of illegally gaining unauthorized entry into computer or computer system. Also the act of circumventing a copy protection scheme.

Cracker   A person who illegally enters or "cracks" into a computer or computer network without proper authorization or consent.

Cryptography   The encrypting of information such a way as to allow only authorized persons to see it.

CyberBullying   The process of insulting, annoying, or threatening another person using a computer, cell phone or the Internet (see also cyber harassment).

Cyber crime   A criminal act in which a computer or the Internet is a vital part of the commission of the crime.

Cyber harassment   The process of insulting, annoying or threatening another person using a computer or the Internet (see also CyberBullying).

CyberCop   A law enforcement officer (LEO) who specializes in computer or Internet related criminal investigations.

Cyberspace   The entire world wide electronic
                               communications system, which includes both
                               small and large computer networks as well as
                               the telephone system.

Daemons   Unix or Linux computer programs, which are
                               tasked to continually run and to provide
                               specific computer or network services.

Dalnet   A large Internet chat computer network. Dalnet
                               is part of the Internet Relay Chat system. See
                               also EFnet.

Decryption   The process of translating computer data or
                               information from a secure and unreadable
                               ("ciphertext") form into a readable format
                               ("plaintext").

Dejanews/Google   An Internet service which logs and archives
                               posting to the many different Internet
                               newsgroups (now owned by Google.
                               groups.google.com

Denial of Service (DOS)   An attack specifically designed to make the
Attack   victims computer unavailable to its user and/or
                               other computers on the Internet.

Dialog box   A graphic rectangle shaped box that provides
                               information to, and receives information from,
                               the computer user.

Direct Client   A process of data transfer from one computer
Connections (DCC)   to another, often seen with Internet Relay Chat
                               (IRC) communications

Discussion groups   A specific Internet meeting, group, topic or
                               bulletin board. Also referred to in Newsgroups.

Disk drive   A computer information storage device. A hard
                               disk drive is the large capacity storage device
                               found in most computers.

Domain Name Address (DNS)
The English-type, human-understandable name for a computer connected to the Internet, such as www.cybercopguide.com.

Domain name extensions
The three-letter extension of a Domain Name address, which assist in explaining the purpose of the computer system. Some of the more popular Domain name extensions include EDU - Educational, GOV - Government, ORG - Non-Profit Organization, COM - Commercial.

DNS
Domain Name System. A method by which IP addresses are converted to human-readable English-type names, and vice versa. (DNS also provides routing information for email and various other internet services.)

DNS Server
A network computer which translates the domain names (such as cyberdetectives.net) into their actual Internet Protocol address (in this case 204.245.198.90).

Dot
The computer term for the period (.) placed between the internet name and IP addresses.

Download
The activity of transferring computer data from another computer system or network to your computer. See also Upload.

DSL modem
A high speed Internet connection device that uses copper wire to transfer data over standard telephone cables.

DVD
A Digital Versatile (Video) Disc in an optical disc used for data storage and video.

Efnet
A large Internet chat computer network. EFnet is part of the Internet Relay Chat system. See also Dalnet.

Email
Electronic Mail. An electronic text message which can be sent from one computer to another via a computer network.

Email address	The electronic location to which a message is sent. An email address is made up of two pieces. The first is the recipient's name (such as Bob). The second part is the domain name of the computer system that you wish to send the message to (such as bob@aol.com). The two parts are separated by a "@" sign (pronounced "at").
Email bomb	A Denial of Service (DOS) attack that involves the sending of thousands of email messages in a short span of time to a victim's email address, thereby depriving him of the legitimate use of his email account.
Email filter	A method of electronically and automatically searching an email as it passes through the computer for certain criteria, such as words or phrases. If the criteria are met, the email can be rerouted or even deleted depending on the user's preferences.
Email header	The often hidden data that is collected by an email as it travels from computer to computer. An email header can be very important in determining the true origin of an email.
Emoticons	Text which is typed in such a way as to create small pictures such as a sideways smiley face :-)
Encryption	The process of translating computer data or information (plaintext) into a secure and unreadable form (ciphertext). The process of translating the information back into a readable form is called decryption.
Ethernet	A physical method of connection computers together into a network. Ethernet was invented as a networking system by the Xerox Corporation.

FAQs (frequently asked questions)	Frequently Asked Questions (FAQs) are articles (usually in the form of electronic text files) which attempt to present the basic information and resources available about a subject.
Federal Bureau of Investigation (FBI)	The FBI is the main investigative arm of the United States Department of Justice (www.fbi.gov)
File	A collection of computer information.
File extension	The three-letter abbreviation used by many computer operating systems to designate the type of file. A file extension of .txt designates text file.
File Transfer Protocol (FTP)	FTP is a type of data transmission protocol commonly used on the Internet to copy files from one computer to another.
Firefox	A web browser by Mozilla (www.mozilla.org)
Firewall	Hardware, software, or a combination of both which act as a security monitor that is designed to allow authorized data transmissions to access a computer network and to prevent unauthorized network access.
Flame	A harsh or angry response, usually via email or chat.
Freeware Software	Computer software that is free of charge to copy and use (see also Public Domain Software).
GIF (Graphics Interchange Format)	A computer graphics format which is characterized as having a custom palette of no more than 256 colors.
Gigabyte (GB)	A measure of computer data. A gigabyte contains roughly 1000 megabytes of data (1024 to be exact).

Gmail	A free email computer system owned by the Google Corporation (www.gmail.com)
Google	A popular Internet search engine (www.google.com). With Google users can search for items on the World Wide Web, including newsgroups postings and images.
Grooming	The process used by people who are sexually attracted to minors (pedophiles) to gain their victim's confidence and loyalty.
Hacker	A person who uses different or unorthodox methods to accomplish a task by tricking a system into doing something it wasn't originally designed to do. A skilled computer programmer. A person who enjoys creating something new, different, or unexpected from something else, thereby pushes the technology beyond its original limits. A person who breaks into computers (a cracker).
Harassment	The repeated act of threatening or annoying a person.
Hard disk drive (HDD)	A large computer storage device which is constructed of one or more magnetic platters on which the data is written to and read from.
Hardware	The physical components of a computer (keyboard, mouse, case, power supply, mother board, etc.)
History folder	The computer data folder which holds the times, dates, and the web sites visited by a person.
Home page	A person's or an organization's main web page (index.htm).
Host	A computer which serves data to another.

Hotmail	A free email computer system owned by the Microsoft Corporation (www.hotmail.com)
HTML (HyperText Markup Language)	The computer programming language, which make up the pages used on the World Wide Web (WWW).
Hyperlink	Text, image or other item on a web page which when clicked takes the user to another location.
Hypertext	An electronic document that contains many different connecting threads. A web page link is a sample of hypertext.
Hypertext link	Text (usually underlined) which when clicked takes the user to another location.
HyperText Transfer Protocol (HTTP)	The standard used for providing web pages on the internet. A web site's Universal Resources locator (URL) begins with HTTP://
ICQ	ICQ (pronounced I-seek-you) is a chat system which allows its users to chat, transfer files, and interact with others around the globe. (www.icq.com)
Information Superhighway	A media term used to describe the worldwide network of computers that are connected via the Internet.
Instant Message (IM)	The chat process used by the AOL instant messenger system to notify a user that a friend (or buddy) is currently online.
Internet Account	A system that a person uses to access the internet. Usually made up of two parts, a user name and a password that is required to utilize the account.
Internet Explorer	A computer application developed by Microsoft that allows computer users to access worldwide web pages.

Internet Filter	A computer program designed to block unwanted or inappropriate information on the Internet.
Internet Hoax	A rumor or information passed around the Internet (usually through email which is held out as fact, but is in reality untrue.) See www.snopes.com
Internet Predator	A person who uses the Internet to take advantage of others, often for their own sexual gratification or financial gain.
Internet Protocol Address (IP address)	The unique numeric number which specifies a particular computer. The IP address for Bob's computer is 192.168.1.2
Internet Relay Chat (IRC)	A large Internet Chat network made up of many different networks. The IRC includes such chat networks as the Dalnet, EFnet and IRCnet.
Internet Service Provider (ISP)	An ISP is a company which provides Internet access to individuals and businesses, usually for a monthly fee. Some of the larger ISPs are Comcast, AT&T, Time Warner, Cox, EarthLink, etc.
Internet Stalking	The process of using the computers and the Internet to repeatedly and without authorization contact, harass, annoy, or frighten another person.
Internet (the Net)	The Internet is the global communication system that links the world's computer networks together. Also referred to as "the Net", "cyberspace", "online", or the "information super highway".
Internet tracking software	Computer software that is designed to monitor and list the Internet activities of another person (www.spectorsoft.com)

IRCnet	A large Internet chat computer network. IRCnet is part of the Internet Relay Chat system. See also Dalnet, EFnet, and IRC.
ISDN	Integrated Services Digital Network- a type of high-speed voice and data network.
Java	A programming language developed by Sun Microsystems. Java is designed so that programs developed on one type of computer will run on another with little or no re-programming of the code.
JPEG (Joint Photographic Experts Group)	A graphic image file format known for its ability to compress large images into files a fraction of the size.
Keywords	A series of words or phrases that a user is searching for. Trees, rain, flowers, Amazon, birds, and animals are keywords associated with the subject "Jungle".
Kiddie porn (KP)	Slang for Child Pornography.
Kilobyte (KB)	A measure of computer data. A kilobyte contains 1024 bytes of data. One kilobyte is roughly the equivalent of one page of single-spaced, typed print.
LAN (Local Area Network)	Two or more computers networked together, usually in the same area or building.
Link	A direct connection between two locations. See also hyperlink.
Listserv	Software or hardware that provides mail lists to a group of people, usually about a particular subject.
Log file	A date file which contains information about computer logins.

Login	The process of entering a computer system. Usually the process includes verification (user name and a password) prior to entry.
Lurker	A person who stays in chat rooms but who does not participate (lurks).
Macintosh	A computer build by Apple Inc., which was the first successful commercial computer to use a graphic user interface (icons, windows, scroll bars, etc.)
Macintosh Operation System	The Operating System (or OS) that runs on the Apple Macintosh computer systems.
Megabyte (MB)	A measure of computer data. A megabyte contains roughly 1000 kilobytes of data (1024 to be exact). One megabyte is the equivalent of roughly 1000 pages of single-spaced typed print.
Megahertz (MHz)	A measurement of a computer processor speed. A million hertz, or a million computer cycles per second equals 1 megahertz (MHz).
MIRC	A popular Windows-based computer program (shareware) written by KhaledMardam-Bey, that allows the user to access the various Internet Relay Chat networks.
Modem	MOdulator-DEModulator. A device used to establish a connection between two computers by transmitting sound waves over standard telephone lines.
Modem jacking	The process where a computer program will take control of the computer's modem and access long distance telephone numbers, often without the knowledge or consent of the computer's owner.
Mouse	An electronic pointing device used to input

hand movements which allows the computer user to control a cursor (or mouse pointer) on the computer screen.

National Center for Missing and Exploited Children (NCMEC)
A non-profit organization started by John Walsh after the abduction of his son, Adam. The NCMEC (www.missingkids.org) helps to locate missing children, provides educational information to parents and law enforcement, and provides an online way to report child exploitation (www.cybertipline.com).

Netiquette
(Network etiquette) The accepted rules and proper courtesy between people who use the Internet. In other words, Internet Manners.

Netizen
A person who uses the internet (InterNETciTIZEN)

Network
Two or more computers linked together to share information.

Newbie
A person who is new to the Internet or new to a particular area of computers.

Newsgroup
An area of the Internet where computer users can place (or post) messages, including text, graphics, photographs, movies and sounds for others to access. The newsgroups are organized by thousands of different subjects.

Office of Juvenile Justice and Delinquency Prevention (OJJDP)
The OJJDP is a Federal program dedicated to assisting state and local communities develop means to prevent and lessen juvenile problems with prevention and intervention programs. The OJJDP website (www.ojjdp.gov) has many free publications designed to educate parents and law enforcement in curbing and preventing the online victimization of children.

Online Predator
A person who uses the Internet to take advantage of others, usually those who are less knowledgeable or experienced then

themselves. Online Predators are most often referred to when speaking of a person who is attempting to locate and assault children using the Internet.

Online Service Provider (OSP)   (see also Internet Service Provider) An organization that provides Internet access along with other information or content.

Operating System (OS)   The software which acts as the interface between the computer user and the computer. The Operating system takes commands given it by the operator and instructs the computer hardware on how to accomplish the request. Microsoft Windows, Mac OS, Unix, and Linux are all types of operating systems.

Outlook   A computer program developed by Microsoft for sending and receiving email. Outlook runs under the Microsoft Windows Operating System.

Packet   A series of characters or "bytes" of data that is sent from one computer to another. On the Internet, information is broken down into smaller "packets" of data and sent from one computer to the next where they are then put back together to form the original data.

Parent Teacher Association (PTA)   A group of local, state, and national educators and parents who work together for the betterment of school children (www.pta.org)

Parental controls   Computer software and/or hardware which allows parents to control some of the types of information that children are exposed to.

Password   A series of letters and or numbers which when placed in the proper sequence, allow a person access to an area that is normally restricted.

PGP   Pretty Good Privacy (PGP). A computer data encryption system created by Phil Zimmerman.

Phreak	Phone fREAK. One who sees the vast telephone system as an interesting and unexplored virtual world that calls out to be explored. One who accesses the telephone networks without proper authorization.
Plaintext	Normal computer data or information before it's encrypted. Also the readable form of data that is produced by the decryption process.
Portable Document File (PDF)	A universal way to create, distribute, read and print electronic documents on many different computers, operating systems, and printers. PDF files are created and can be read by using the Adobe Acrobat software written by Adobe systems, Inc. (www.adobe.com)
Pornography	Images or photographs of people over the age of 18 engaging in sexually explicit activities (see also Child Pornography).
Post	An electronic message that has been placed by someone to a web page, a blog, newsgroups or other portion of the Internet.
Posting	The act of placing an electronic message to the Internet, newsgroups or other online group.
Processor	An integrated circuit which is the central processing unit (CPU) for a computer.
Program	A series of electronic instructions which when run perform a function on a computer (a word processor such as Microsoft Word is a program).
Public Domain Software	Computer software that not covered by copyright and considered free of charge to copy and use (see also Freeware and Shareware).
RAM (Random Access	A type of computer memory in which each

Memory)	character of data can be quickly and specifically accessed by the computer. The more RAM a computer has the more information that it can hold and the faster it can process the required data.
Real time	An activity on a computer or the internet which occurs immediately and without any waiting.
Removable disks	Computer storage devices which allow the user to take the data and move it to another location. Floppy disks, Thumb drives, CDR/CDRW and DVDs are considered removable disks.
Scanning, Port Scanning	The act of using a computer to look at the computer ports of another computer on a network. Port Scanner software can be used by legitimate network system administrators to test and check computer on their network. Scanner software can also be used by people who are looking to see if a computer has open and unsecured ports as a first step into attempting to gain unauthorized access to someone else's computer (cracking).
Screen name	The alias, "handle", or "nic" (NICkname) or other moniker that a person uses while on the Internet. Screen name first became popular with America Online Users who needed a screen name to send and receive email as well as for purposes of chatting. A screen name allows people some anonymity while on the Internet.
Search engine	An internet computer program or web site that allows a user to quickly and more easily search the millions of Internet sites for information.
Search engine filter	A method that Internet Search Engines uses to keep unwanted information from being shown in the results of Internet search requests. Many Internet search engines now including filtering

in an attempt to keep users from seeing unwanted or inappropriate material.

Search warrant   An order by a Judge which allows law enforcement to gain access to a person, place or item so that it may be searched and/or seized as part of a criminal investigation.

Server   A computer which is programmed to accept requests for information and to provide (or serve) that information to authorized users. Servers provide web sites (web servers), emails (email servers) and other Internet activities.

Sexting   (Sex + Texting) Using the text messaging or other forms of electronic communication to send and receive sexual written messages, images, and video between people.

Shareware   Computer software which is distributed freely, but if used requires payment of a fee to the author or company that owns it (see Freeware and Public Domain Software.

Smart phone   A cellular telephone with extended capabilities including Internet Access and applications.

Snail mail   The physical process of writing, mailing and delivering a letter, by using such services as the U.S. Postal Service, FedEx, UPS, DHL, etc.

Social Networking site   An Internet site and method for a group or groups of people who gather together electronically and share information with each other.

Software   The computer Operating System (OS), computer programs, and other electronic computer programs that instruct a computer on what it is to do.

Spam	Unwanted or unsolicited commercial email. The Internet term for Spam is rumored to have been a reference to a Monty Python comedy skit about Vikings and a restaurant serving the luncheon meat called Spam.
Spammer	A person who send out unwanted or unsolicited email (Spam).
Stalk, stalking	The ongoing and repeated process of contacting another person without their consent. Some states definitions of stalking also require that the person is in fear by the person trying to repeatedly contact them.
Subscribe	The act of requesting membership or acceptance into a service, such as a monthly Internet email service, a web site, or other group.
Surf or surfing	The act of using a computer to access the Internet. Surfing is often defined as using a web browser to access the World Wide Web (WWW); however any Internet activity, newsgroups, chat, etc. can be considered "surfing" the Internet.
Telnet	A program or a command that allows a person to directly connect from one computer to another using text based commands.
TIFF (Tag Image File Format)	A computer image file format which uses data compression to storage large images in millions of colors.
Thumbdrive	A small USB storage device capable of containing large amounts of information.
Traceroute	The command that allows a user on the Internet to see the path that data takes as it moves along the network from one computer to another.

Trojan Horse	A computer program or computer data that appears to be one thing, but contains a hidden program inside - one that could potentially cause damage to the victim's computer.
U.S. Customs & Border Protection	United States Customs and Border Protection is the primary enforcement agency protecting the Nation's borders. The also investigate child pornography and the unlawful exploitation of children (www.CBP.gov).
U.S. Secret Service	The United States Secret Service is the primary enforcement agency protecting against counterfeit currency and for protection of the President and other dignitaries. (www.secretservice.gov)
Undernet	A large Internet chat computer network. Undernet is part of the Internet Relay Chat system. See also Dalnet.
Uniform Resource Locator (URL)	The method of specifying a location for information on the Internet. For example the URL for the National Center for Missing and Exploited Children is http://www.missingkids.org.
Unix	A computer Operating System developed in the late 60s by Bell Laboratories.
Unsolicited email	Unwanted electronic mail (email). See also Spam.
Upload	The activity of transferring computer data from your computer to another computer system or network. See also Download.
Usenet	The thousands of different newsgroups or discussion forums accessed via the Internet (see also Newsgroups).
User name	A persons Internet account name (see also Screen Name), often requiring a password to

gain entry into an account.

Virus An unwanted computer program which attempts to attach itself to a person's computer software, usually without the user's knowledge or consent. A computer virus often acts much like it's organic counterpart in that many of them attempt to replicate themselves and move from computer to computer in an attempt to infect as many computers as possible.

Vulnerability Scanner A computer program designed to examine a computer or computer network which can then attempt to penetrate the security or the target machine(s).

Warez The illegal buying, selling, trading and acquisition of stolen computer software (also referred to a pirating or software piracy).

Web Cache The area or folder where an Internet web browser stores the web pages, text and graphics from previous web sessions.

Web history The file where the location of previous web sites are listed.

Web page Visual file of text and/or graphics which are found on the World Wide Web (WWW) and displayed on the user's computer screen.

Website The web page or pages that are provided the World Wide Web pages via a computer called a web server (see also Server).

Whois The Internet/Unix type command or program that lists the registered owner of a web site on the World Wide Web (WWW).

Windows Operating System The operating system (OS) developed by Microsoft which is characterized by is graphical user interface by use of graphic icons and windows.

Wire tapping	The process of secretly obtaining information in real time without a person's knowledge or consent.
World Wide Web (WWW)	The millions of computer and Internet sites that provide web pages to computer users using web-browsing software.
WYSIWYG	Acronym for "What You See Is What You Get". This indicates that whatever you see on the computer screen is what you will receive when printed or given to someone else.
Yahoo!	A large Internet Web Site and search engine which provides a wide variety of Internet services including free email, web pages, maps, chat, shopping, and more (www.yahoo.com)

Appendix C - Internet International Country Codes

AC - Ascension Island
AD - Andorra
AE - United Arab Emirates
AF - Afghanistan
AG - Antigua and Barbuda
AI - Anguilla
AL - Albania
AM - Armenia
AN - Netherlands Antilles
AO - Angola
AQ - Antarctica
AR - Argentina
AS - American Samoa
AT - Austria
AU - Australia
AW - Aruba
AZ - Azerbaijan
BA - Bosnia and Herzegovina
BB - Barbados
BD - Bangladesh
BE - Belgium
BF - Burkina Faso
BG - Bulgaria
BH - Bahrain
BI - Burundi
BJ - Benin
BM - Bermuda
BN - Brunei Darussalam
BO - Bolivia
BR - Brazil
BS - Bahamas
BT - Bhutan
BV - Bouvet Island
BW - Botswana
BY - Belarus
BZ - Belize
CA - Canada
CC - Cocos (Keeling) Islands

CD - Democratic Republic of Congo (formerly Zaire)
CF - Central African Republic
CG - Congo
CH - Switzerland
CI - Cote D'Ivoire (Ivory Coast)
CK - Cook Islands
CL - Chile
CM - Cameroon
CN - China
CO - Colombia
CR - Costa Rica
CS - Czechoslovakia (former)
CU - Cuba
CV - Cape Verde
CX - Christmas Island
CY - Cyprus
CZ - Czech Republic
DE - Germany
DJ - Djibouti
DK - Denmark
DM - Dominica
DO - Dominican Republic
DZ - Algeria
EC - Ecuador
EE - Estonia
EG - Egypt
EH - Western Sahara
ER - Eritrea
ES - Spain
ET - Ethiopia
FI - Finland
FJ - Fiji
FK - Falkland Islands (Malvinas)
FM - Micronesia
FO - Faroe Islands
FR - France
FX - France, Metropolitan
GA - Gabon
GB - Great Britain (UK)
GD - Grenada
GE - Georgia
GF - French Guiana
GH - Ghana

GI - Gibraltar
GL - Greenland
GM - Gambia
GN - Guinea
GP - Guadeloupe
GQ - Equatorial Guinea
GR - Greece
GS - S. Georgia & S. Sandwich Islands
GT - Guatemala
GU - Guam
GW - Guinea-Bissau
GY - Guyana
HK - Hong Kong
HM - Heard and McDonald Islands
HN - Honduras
HR - Croatia (Hrvatska)
HT - Haiti
HU - Hungary
ID - Indonesia
IE - Ireland
IL - Israel
IN - India
IO - British Indian Ocean Territory
IQ - Iraq
IR - Iran
IS - Iceland
IT - Italy
JM - Jamaica
JO - Jordan
JP - Japan
KE - Kenya
KG - Kyrgyzstan
KH - Cambodia
KI - Kiribati
KM - Comoros
KN - Saint Kitts and Nevis
KP - Korea (North)
KR - Korea (South)
KW - Kuwait
KY - Cayman Islands
KZ - Kazakhstan
LA - Laos
LB - Lebanon

LC - Saint Lucia
LI - Liechtenstein
LK - Sri Lanka
LR - Liberia
LS - Lesotho
LT - Lithuania
LU - Luxembourg
LV - Latvia
LY - Libya
MA - Morocco
MC - Monaco
MD - Moldova
MG - Madagascar
MH - Marshall Islands
MK - Macedonia
ML - Mali
MM - Myanmar
MN - Mongolia
MO - Macau
MP - Northern Mariana Islands
MQ - Martinique
MR - Mauritania
MS - Montserrat
MT - Malta
MU - Mauritius
MV - Maldives
MW - Malawi
MX - Mexico
MY - Malaysia
MZ - Mozambique
NA - Namibia
NC - New Caledonia
NE - Niger
NF - Norfolk Island
NG - Nigeria
NI - Nicaragua
NL - Netherlands
NO - Norway
NP - Nepal
NR - Nauru
NT - Neutral Zone
NU - Niue
NZ - New Zealand (Aotearoa)

OM - Oman
PA - Panama
PE - Peru
PF - French Polynesia
PG - Papua New Guinea
PH - Philippines
PK - Pakistan
PL - Poland
PM - St. Pierre and Miquelon
PN - Pitcairn
PR - Puerto Rico
PT - Portugal
PW - Palau
PY - Paraguay
QA - Qatar
RE - Reunion
RO - Romania
RU - Russia
RW - Rwanda
SA - Saudi Arabia
SB - Solomon Islands
SC - Seychelles
SD - Sudan
SE - Sweden
SG - Singapore
SH - St. Helena
SI - Slovenia
SJ - Svalbard and Jan Mayen Islands
SK - Slovak Republic
SL - Sierra Leone
SM - San Marino
SN - Senegal
SO - Somalia
SR - Surinam
ST - Sao Tome and Principe
SV - El Salvador
SY - Syria
SZ - Swaziland
TC - Turks and Caicos Islands
TD - Chad
TF - French Southern Territories
TG - Togo
TH - Thailand

TJ - Tajikistan
TK - Tokelau
TM - Turkmenistan
TN - Tunisia
TO - Tonga
TP - East Timor
TR - Turkey
TT - Trinidad and Tobago
TV - Tuvalu
TW - Taiwan
TZ - Tanzania
UA - Ukraine
UG - Uganda
UK - United Kingdom
UM - US Minor Outlying Islands
US - United States
UY - Uruguay
UZ - Uzbekistan
VA - Vatican City State (Holy See)
VC - Saint Vincent and the Grenadines
VE - Venezuela
VG - Virgin Islands (British)
VI - Virgin Islands (U.S.)
VN - Viet Nam
VU - Vanuatu
WF - Wallis and Futuna Islands
WS - Samoa
YE - Yemen
YT - Mayotte
YU - Yugoslavia
ZA - South Africa
ZM - Zambia
ZR - Zaire (now CD - Democratic Republic of Congo)
ZW - Zimbabwe
COM - Global (Commercial)
EDU - USA (Educational)
GOV - USA (Government)
INT - International
MIL - USA (Military)
NET - Global (Network)
ORG - Global (Non-Profit Organization
PRO - Professional Services

Index

A

Acceptable Use Policy, 266, 273
Adium, 26
Agent, 34, 49, 177, 181, 239
alt.binaries, 48
alt.sex, 48
Anarchists, 64, 244
AOL, 25, 31, 113, 127, 273, 275, 283
AOL Instant Messenger, 25, 31, 273
ARPAnet, 5
Avast, 124
AVG, 124, 233, 234
Azureus, 44

B

Bearshare, 43
Binary Boy, 49, 274
Bing, 63, 83, 85, 86, 131
Bitcomet, 44
BitTorrent, 42, 43, 206
bmp, 168
bomb, 65, 111, 192, 244, 245, 280
Bomb recipes, 64, 244
Bsecure, 86

C

cell phone, 23, 53, 129, 149, 202, 209, 210
cell phones, 15, 51, 102, 209, 210
Chat, 10, 23, 25, 27, 32, 34, 37, 127, 128, 152, 156, 213, 238, 276, 278, 279, 284, 285, 286, 293
child pornography, 49, 57, 128, 168, 177, 182, 209, 211, 213, 214
Child Pornography, 210
Chrome, 9, 11, 75, 101
Computer Intrusion, 219, 249, 277
Computer Viruses, 224
cookie, 76, 77, 78, 79, 81, 84, 108, 169, 277
Counterfeiting, 257
Craigslist, 137
Credit Cards, 247
Cyber Bullying, 137, 142
Cyber Patrol, 86
CyberBullying, 191
Cybersitter, 107
CyberSitter, 86
cyberspace, 5
cyber-stalking, 137

D

Dateline, viii, 128, 187
Denial of Service, 225, 238, 240, 278, 280
Denial of Service Attacks, 225
Digsby, 26
Direct Client Connections, 32, 278
Domain Name Server, 12
Domain Name Services, 101
Domain Names Services, 101
DSL, 6, 9, 279
DSL modem, 6

E

Email, 15, 24, 111, 116, 117, 118, 125, 261, 280

F

Facebook, 19, 20, 23, 24, 28, 123, 129
Family Safety, 88, 90, 91, 92, 93, 95, 96, 99, 102, 107
FamilySafety, 88
FBI, 34, 35, 36, 39, 212, 213, 214, 255, 281
File Sharing, 41, 42, 206
Firefox, 9, 11, 12, 15, 69, 75, 101
Firewall, 233
Frostwire, 43

G

Gavin De Becker, 14
gif, 168, 171
Gmail, 15, 16, 17, 24, 113, 137
Gnutella, 42, 43
Google, 21, 24, 25, 48, 63, 75, 83, 84,
    85, 101, 113, 131, 142, 178, 278,
    282
Google+, 24
GooglePlus, 23

H

hacking, 219
Hacking, 219
Hangouts, 24
Happyman, 176, 178, 179, 180, 181,
    182, 183, 184, 185
harassment, 53, 137, 138, 139, 140,
    143, 144, 146, 191, 195, 277, 282
Harassment, 142, 191
Hate Sites, 63, 243
Hotmail, 15, 17, 24, 88, 113, 120, 137,
    160, 192, 194, 266, 282, 283

I

ICQ, 25, 229, 283
information super highway, 5
Internet Country Codes, 8
Internet Explorer, 9, 11, 12, 15, 16, 69,
    70, 73, 74, 75, 76, 79, 81, 101, 275,
    283
Internet Filtering, 83, 87, 104
Internet Filters, 83
Internet History, 73
Internet Protocol Address, 7, 284
Internet Relay Chat, 213
Internet Service Provider, 5, 6, 9, 101,
    103, 104, 109, 117, 120, 123, 125,
    150, 167, 194, 198, 203, 214, 226,
    235, 250, 251, 254, 255, 256, 284,
    288
Ipchicken, 9
IRC, 32, 33, 34, 128, 156, 213, 278,
    284, 285

Ircle, 32

J

JPEG, 168, 171, 285
jpg, 168, 171, 173, 174, 175

L

Limewire, 43
LimeWire, 43

M

Macintosh, 11, 32, 107, 286
Microsoft Windows, 11, 170, 288
mIRC, 26, 32
Missing Children, 147
Multimedia Messaging Service, 209
Myspace, 21, 123
Myyearbook, 21

N

Napster, 41
National Center for Missing and
    Exploited Children, 149, 271, 287,
    293
NCMEC, 149, 287
Net Nanny, 86, 107
newsgroup, 47, 48, 49, 124, 243
Newsgroups, 10, 47, 48, 49, 57, 124,
    187, 274, 278, 293
Nickelodeon, 7, 12, 13
Norton Anti-Virus, 124

O

OpenDNS, 101, 102, 267
Opera, 12, 275
Outlook, 48, 288

P

packets, 13, 288
Passwords, 249

Phex, 43
PIRCH, 32
pornography, 38, 48, 50, 57, 58, 61, 62,
    66, 108, 111, 123, 128, 142, 157,
    158, 159, 167, 168, 176, 177, 178,
    179, 181, 185, 201, 204, 206, 207,
    209, 211, 212, 213, 214, 215, 218,
    253, 273, 276, 289, 293
Pornography, 61, 201, 206, 210, 211,
    271, 285, 289
Property Crimes, 247

R

Runaway, 147, 151

S

Safari, 11
SafeSearch, 84, 85
Scanners, 221
Search Engine Filters, 83
sexting, 209, 210
Sexting, 209
Shareaza, 44
Skype, 23, 24, 25
Social Networking, 19, 134
Spam, 111, 117, 123, 292, 293
Spectorsoft, 107
Stalking, 143, 284

T

Theft, 247, 249
tif, 168
TIFF, 168, 292
Tracking Software, 83, 107
Trillian, 26
Trojan horse, 45, 124, 222, 225, 233
Trojan Horses, 222

Twitter, 26
TYFLAS, 182, 183, 184

U

unsolicited email, 117, 123, 124, 125,
    292
Usenet, 47, 293
utorrent, 44

V

Virus Protection, 232
Vuze, 44

W

Web Caches, 69, 113
Web Histories, 69, 113
Whois, 140, 142, 294
Windows Live, 25, 88, 89, 90, 91, 92,
    93, 95, 99, 107
World Wide Web, 11, 12, 13, 14, 15,
    16, 19, 41, 53, 61, 66, 69, 85, 124,
    140, 147, 155, 172, 187, 221, 234,
    266, 269, 271, 275, 277, 282, 283,
    292, 294, 295

Y

Yahoo, 15, 24, 25, 27, 28, 31, 33, 63,
    113, 128, 131, 137, 160, 178, 266,
    295
Yahoo Instant Messenger, 27, 28

Z

Zoobuh, 115, 116

14999406R00169

Made in the USA
Lexington, KY
02 May 2012